METAPSYCHOLOGY
OF THE
CREATIVE PROCESS

Continuous Novelty as the
Ground of Creative Advance

Jason W. Brown

ia

imprint-academic.com

Published in the UK by
Imprint Academic, PO Box 200, Exeter EX5 5YX, UK

Distributed in the USA by
Ingram Book Company,
One Ingram Blvd., La Vergne, TN 37086, USA

ISBN 9781845409234

A CIP catalogue record for this book is available from the
British Library and US Library of Congress

Contents

God guard me from those thoughts men think
In the mind alone
He that sings a lasting song
Thinks in the marrow-bone.
      —W.B. Yeats, 1935, *A Prayer for Old Age*

Preface

Many are fascinated by the phenomenon of genius and search for an understanding of its nature, a frustrating endeavor since the inability to "get inside the head" of a creative individual, and the mystery, at times fragility, of the process, even to those most gifted, as well as their common reluctance to describe it, even if they could, leaves one to focus on extrinsic conditions associated with giftedness, such as life experience, IQ, genetic endowment, heritance, neurotic disorder or temperament, alcoholism, birth order and so on, all of interest but none that shed light on the inner process of the creative imagination. Researchers are like the proverbial blind men describing an elephant. Such factors influence the creative but are not especially helpful in elucidating the inner process or its relation to ordinary thought.

Psychoanalysis is perhaps the only theory that has addressed specific aspects of personality development and the structure of the unconscious, which is the undoubted source of the creative imagination, but psychoanalysis is a theory of deviation with a tendency to apply formulaic and not widely credible interpretations to the behavior of all individuals without a clear path from normalcy and deviance to giftedness. The present work also comes from clinical studies, but of focal brain injuries that dissect unconscious cognition to reveal sub-surface lines of processing. The outcome is a process (microgenetic) theory of the mental state that differs markedly from the substantialist and externalist foundations of mainstream (cognitive) psychology, but with the potential to clarify many features of thought and imagery, normal and exceptional. A summary of the main lines of the theory is included as an addendum to this book.

Creativity is not an isolated problem but touches many central issues in philosophical psychology. The creative is juxtaposed to the habitual as a departure from convention and routine, to the causal as an original construct that is not explained by necessity, to complexity, contingency and probability by order and coherence, and to machine theory by the centrality of feeling (in art) and the intrinsic relation of the emotive and the conceptual, all topics that constitute a metapsychology of thought.[1]

The principle aim of this book is to explore the continuum from novelty in nature and the evolutionary process to the highest forms of creativity in human experience, with a focus on the subjectivity of intra-psychic process in relation to the adaptive constraints of sensibility. The truly creative is subsurface cognition parsed by necessity to a meaningful outcome in the world. Microgenetic theory has the capacity to illuminate some of the obscurities in the transmutation of objects of fantasy and imagination, the elicitation of conscious material from unconscious categories, and the conveyance of feeling to others. I would point out that I have departed from the process-theoretical account of Creativity as a universal or absolute, and novelty as an occasion of change, conceiving uniform novelty as a feature of change in dissolution or advance that is tapped to a varying degree in the creative imagination.

I would be remiss not to mention the invaluable commentaries on my work by David Bradford and the years of friendship with Marcel Kinsbourne, two highly creative spirits in neuropsychology, the assistance of Maria Pachalaska in editing the manuscript, the encouragement of John Cobb, the contact with, and writings of, the late Timothy Sprigge, but most of all the beauty and tranquility of my home in Provence, the site of annual conferences in process thought (to be collected shortly by Michel Weber), and an idyllic locale for a writer, all owing to

---

[1]   Preliminary efforts to explore this topic are in Brown (1997; 1999; 2008). A recent account of the process model with citations is Brown (2015).

my darling wife, Carine, my loving companion and spiritual guide over these many years.

Chapter 1

Introduction

Who would study and describe the living starts,
By driving the spirit out of its parts.[2]
— *Goethe, Faust, Part 1*

Historically, there are two paths into the topic of creativity, each quite independent of the other. One approach concerns novelty in acts and ideas, ranging from the activities of everyday life to the products of artistic and scientific thought, the other, metaphysics. Ordinarily, these two ways of thinking about creativity, one psychological, the other philosophical, do not share a common ground but are conceived as distinct problems. The aim of this work is to demonstrate that a process psychology of mind offers a different way of conceptualizing both approaches as a step toward their unification, bringing into relation the continuum of passage in nature to a transition from repetition to innovation to genius. The theory that governs this inquiry, the process-model of the mind/brain state (Brown, 2015, for review), described in relation to normal and pathological cognition, as well as to aesthetic, moral and religious thought, and compatible arguments in process philosophy, serves as an organizing principle for diverse manifestations of creative process beginning with individual mind and the correlated brain state, with an inferred continuum from process underlying thought and behavior to process in material

---

[2]   The citation is:
"Wer will das Lebendigs erkennen und beschreiben,
Suchts erst den Geist herauszutreiben."

nature, of which human creativity is, so far as we know, the highest, most refined exemplification.

Many have the idea that high levels of creativity, or successive grades of genius, are inaccessible and beyond the comprehension of scholars, opaque even to the gifted themselves who often describe their own work in terms of a relation to ordinary cognition. For Rousseau, every individual has the potential for genius. Darwin wrote that he was quite ordinary in most respects, even slower than his friends. Edison's 99% perspiration is another example. The relation to ordinary cognition is seen indirectly in creativity during intoxication and transitional or trance-states such as Wagner's dream (described in *Mein Leben*) of the inspired music of the *Prelude* to *Das Rheingold* or the opiate trance in which Coleridge composed *Kublai Khan* (examples in Koestler, 1964). I recall an interview with a celebrated composer who, when asked the impolitic question of why so much of his work was trivial, replied that it was necessary to produce a few works of lasting value. The attribution of creativity to an extrinsic muse or inspiration, or a mysterious intrinsic source in the unconscious, implies that even the gifted are unaware of the origin of their endowment. Many are anxious that they will lose a creative ability that seems to come from nowhere, endures blocks and dry spells, and cannot be facilitated by effort. Another factor pointing to a relation to ordinary thought is the high level of preparedness required, which is devoted to one domain of cognition, and charged by happenstance. This agrees with the observation that most people are extraordinarily creative in dream — Goethe's "pool of the creative unconscious" — but in only a few does this carry over into wakefulness.

To the extent that creativity in human affairs has been a topic for philosophical reflection, it has been conceived as imaginative play, mental activity that is divinely or otherwise inspired (e.g. Plato), a complex interplay of ecstatic intoxication with sober restraint (Nietzsche), imagination modulated by real world constraints, unconscious constructs channeled through conscious rationality (Freud) or, more generally, reason and adaptive values applied to the products of fantasy. Clearly, philosophical analysis is burdened by the prominence of affect, individuality and the import of personal experience, as well as the non-rationality of artistic thought. There is also the role of intuition in mathematical discovery (Poincaré) as in other modes of thought, of visual imagery (Einstein) and, more generally, by the paradox of something appearing from nothing, and the conflict of novelty with causation. Various methods of study include personality profiles, psychometric testing, genetic, familial and cultural influences. Genius is often a guide to lesser modes of originality or, in the case of Darwin, as a model for the creative process (Simonton, 1999[3]). The life-history and behavioral patterns of gifted individuals are of great importance, as documented in the essay on "Jocasta Mothering" by Besdine (1971).[4]

Speculation also tends to focus on the distinction of creativity from adjacent concepts (originality, innovation, etc.), and the relation of intuition and spontaneity to reason and deliberation. What is most pronounced in the subjectivity of art differs from the objectivity of science, for example, the resolution in art of individuality and taste compared to, in science, collaboration and consensus, or in the latter, the difference of theory and experiment, or competence (technique, skill) and performance. One must also resolve those ideas that are sudden and felt as inspired with those that are incremental. The receptivity of early experience contrasts with the agency of later preparation, and instances when discovery seems accidental, such as Fleming's discovery of penicillin, or Kekule's snake dream that inspired the benzene ring.

The potential for creativity in many individuals has to be reconciled with the role (at least nominal) of the heritability of intelligence and its presumed relation to creative work, especially in science, as well as precocity (Gauss, Mozart). An unconscious origin conforms to the (generally agreed) necessity for years of study, accumulated knowledge, mastery of craft or technique and relevant personal or professional experience. If

---

[3]   This is an exceptional review of the various factors that influence creativity.

[4]   See the collection in Paul and Kaufman (2014) for discussion of contemporary issues in the study of creativity. Also, Brown (1997; 2008) for prior discussions of creativity, mysticism and metaphor.

creativity is, *inter alia*, an emphasis on certain attributes of the self, e.g. a creative personality, including knowledge, confidence, assuredness and experiential memory, these would still be incidental to the mentality of the self in a creative act. As to historical and cultural aspects, James noted that individual creativity is rarely an isolated phenomenon but occurs in a context and tradition. A good example is the extraordinary burst of genius in Periclean Athens, Elizabethan London, and turn-of-the-nineteenth- and twentieth-century Vienna. Yet, it is also true, as Gray wrote, that:

> Full many a flow'r is born to blush unseen,
> And waste its sweetness on the desert air.

Accounts by creative individuals on the development and realization of concepts and skills are by and large anecdotal, since the infrastructure of the creative act is concealed from the artist no less than from the analyst. There is emphasis on holistic thinking, immediacy of grasp and, commonly, a description of the act as passive, with the artist a recipient rather than an agent, like a scribe to god's dictation. Discipline is essential but effort does not help. Eckermann wrote of Goethe that genius does not struggle to achieve the heights, genius soars.

Conscious thought and the feeling of agency may be more emphatic in scientific work than in art, since novel ideas must be vetted by co-workers and the wider scientific community. Progress is usually incremental and within the tradition of the field. Science builds on factual knowledge, which is not especially relevant to art. There is also the impression of a race to discovery in which one individual or team is first at the finish line, as with the polio vaccine or DNA. This is true even at the highest levels; for example, Darwin and Wallace, Newton and Leibniz and the infinite calculus, or Einstein and Whitehead on relativity theory, and leads to the supposition that, for the most part, scientific discovery, at least in modern times and except for precedence, does not so much reveal the signature of the scientist as that of teams of co-workers, in contrast to an individuality of artistic style and the unique "voice" of the artist. We think of science as fact- or tradition-based and art as an often radical departure from convention, but the most powerful minds in art and science—a Beethoven, Newton—sum up the preceding epoch and incorporate its paradigms (Kuhn, 1962) even as they transform the field to a novel perspective.

The creative is one facet of the novelty that, more deeply, governs passage and advance. Novelty within and across epochal states, in mind and nature, eludes observation because it is uniform. What is common to all escapes detection. From this standpoint, novelty in the momentary transition of mental states and creativity in gifted individuals exemplify a process ingredient in psyche and nature. Novelty is a universal feature of passage and a covert property of change. On this view, certain individuals, to a greater or lesser extent, are vehicles or propagators through which inherent novelty becomes manifest. This is in keeping with the passive quality of creative ideas, their unconscious origin and the sense of an external agency. Giftedness is receptivity to universal novelty, implemented in the activity of the brain, with genius an exceptional sensitivity to the creativity of natural process, the capacity to raise novelty to a conceptual level, and to convey in actuality works of exceptional power and beauty. Genius is not divine but the comparison is apt in the sampling and realization of the creativity of nature that is, arguably, the mind of god.

If artistic genius is the paradigm—the works of Beethoven or Shakespeare, for example—the only parallel is to men of philosophical or scientific genius—Plato, Newton, Einstein—who did not merely solve complex problems or uncover secrets but, like the great artists, created a world. Here, the process of scientific and artistic creativity may be similar. At a lesser stage, art is an individual endeavor of personality and feeling, which would be considered inappropriate in science, lacking an attempt at rationality, proof, collaboration, adherence to tradition, and rapid obsolescence of ideas,[5] which appeal to a narrow and skilled group of colleagues. For the most part, science is about problem-solving or the discovery of nature's

---

[5]   In art, works go in and out of fashion, while in science they are, for the most part, destined to be replaced.

secrets, not personal invention. Art has connoisseurs but is meant to appeal to a public, not the halls of the academy. We mourn the early death of a great composer such as Schubert, for we know that no one would have composed works left undone by his untimely death. In science, it is a race to get there first since most scientific discoveries would, in time, have been made by others.

In contrast, there is little attention to the mental process(es) underlying creative thought, not surprising given that conventional accounts of mind, especially stimulus-response theory and mechanical interaction, as in circuit-board or computational models, leave no path into novelty except for a compilation of reflex-like operations or the invocation of greater complexity. This near-hegemonic theory of mind is by its nature antithetical to the creative act. A level of absurdity was reached when Guillford (1980) proposed up to 180 relevant components, though his concept of "divergent" and "convergent" thinking is most often cited. Creativity (or novelty), its coherence or its illogic, conceptual advance and unpredictability, would seem to depend on acausal features of cognition, not mere recombination, and far from being resolved by computational theory provide evidence against it, if in no other respect than the assumption of unconscious cognition, emotional factors, unpredictability and surprise.

Moreover, arguments that creativity is computational or combinatorial must explain how complexity or recombination leads to novel concepts, not only to genius, but to coherence. In artistic creation the primacy and transmission of feeling is a challenge to philosophical interpretation, as well as the non-rational constructs that go into the production and enjoyment of an artwork. There is also the problem of what accounts for giftedness in a chosen few and conventional thinking in others? A computer fed the fables of Montaigne or the music of Bach might produce minimally novel instances of each artwork,[6] but

---

6   This actually happened some years ago at a conference in Venice, when a
     computer version of a fable similar to those of Aesop, Tolstoy or Montaigne
     was presented by a leading figure in this field without taking into account
     programming the computer with like instances.

this is no more than simulation and does not account for the original idea. Should the computer be fed with all the music written *prior* to Bach, or music to which Bach is known to have had access, and then, *sans* Bach, produce a Bach-like masterpiece, that would be more convincing.

To the extent that mental process is the target of inquiry, the tendency is to distinguish different modes of thought, or kinds and degrees of imagination: fancy, play, trial action, openness, transitional-states and the relation to psychopathology. For the most part, discussion centers around a generalization of relevant process — metaphor, insight, diligence, openness — or a focus on traits common to gifted individuals, the contexts and predispositions that frame discovery, or the role of cultural, historical and developmental patterns, most of which do not directly address mind/brain process and its deviation, or derivation, from process in nature. The wide scope of approaches is itself evidence of the absence of an accepted theory that could ground and inform a study of the creative process.

Some ideas that merit attention in this respect are (1) the role of potential (wholes) in generating alternative possibilities (parts), (2) the centrality of derailment in the normal course of thought, not merely a deviation from the predictable but conceptual propagation as in metaphor, paralogic, syncretic thought, and free imagery, and (3) the deviation from habit or expectation at deep, or early, phases in the mental state, such that the earlier the derailment, the wider, more generic and inclusive the idea, while the later the derailment, the more specific and definite the outcome. However, the exploration of conceptual depth, category boundaries, overlap of successive states and part/whole relations are not dispositive, for novel concepts can be irrelevant, banal or incoherent. Truly creative work requires a detachment from the ordinary that is informed by learning, skill, technique and knowledge of the relevant field. Generally, the more confined the conceptual frame, as in science, logic or mathematics, the more discrete and specialized the creative product. Kant argued that philosophy, including his own, was not creative, and Sprigge echoed this opinion, writing that a new idea in philosophy was almost certain to be wrong.

1. Animal Behavior and Human Mind

An animal confronted by a predator may run, freeze, seek shelter or concealment, each behavior determined by subtle changes in the relation of prey to predator. Further, within each response there are multiple possibilities none of which are latent, pre-wired and awaiting activation. Responses are not *in situ* prior to selection, they are not-yet-existent possibilities embedded in a potential—category—for a variety of possible actions. A similar inventory of actions, some relatively fixed, others opportunistic, occur in feeding, mating and other drive-based activities. Within a limited number of scenarios the variety of behavior implies potential in a category, not a reflex-like automatism.

Compare this with the mind of a novelist, in whom there is a similar, if much wider, range of options—plots, characters—that take shape on realization. In some writers this is a gradual unfolding of the hoped-for outcome; in others, it is deliberate, stepwise and conscious; in a rare few, it is worked out in advance. An example of limited composition prior to writing is Milton who, blind, composed a verse each day and later dictated it for transcription. But in all creative individuals, whether spontaneous or conscious, whether fact-based or fantasy, the progression from potential to actual with varying degrees of forethought is very much a surfacing of ideas and words out of an unconscious source in which the micro-temporal transition is opaque to thought. One moment there is little more than a contact or disposition, the next a novel idea or phrase. Along with the magic of discovery, which is a revelation of varying degrees of depth, the usual lack of a feeling of agency gives a sense of fragility to the creative gift. On completing a novel, many writers fear it will be their last.

In the instance of animal mind when instinct predominates, the actualization of drive is modulated by experience. There is no boundary of conscious and unconscious, yet the transition from source to actuality is no less obscure than in the human mind. In the writer, ideas are generated out of potential in, or into, the imagination, where they are mulled over, sorted out, propagate and/or transferred to the page. The writer may have the impression of deciding among options but one could as readily claim that the options are given in such a way that what survives in a written text conforms to a feeling of "rightness", which resolves external necessity with internal context. The artistic or scientific product must satisfy thought and adapt to reality. In art, the conformance is closer to thought; in science, it is closer to fact. The finality in consciousness is an assimilation, not an output. The author finds justification in choices that are not made but uncovered.

In line with this approach, Bosanquet wrote that the creative idea in drawing is concentrated at the tip of the pen; the final image is not in the mind until the drawing is complete. Even a writer who composes in the imagination before committing the idea to literary or scientific formulation will have an involuntary feeling. One might go so far as to say that the quality of the creative product reflects the lack of volition in evoking and reviving the creative idea. In both animal and author, the product is realized out of a background category, in one case relating to instinct or drive, in the other, to the drive-derivatives of desire and affect-ideas. Wittgenstein wrote that thought begins with instinct. Every thought arises as intentional feeling or desire out of precursor instincts. In the animal, the process is direct; in the writer, it passes through a phase of imagery. Yet in both, the act is instigated prior to final exactitude. One can say, the animal makes an implicit choice, not a decision. The writer decides, or more likely a decision is presented beforehand, in ongoing thought or in later revision.[7] The experience of the animal plays a role in what seems to be an automatic choice, just as experiential knowledge plays a role in the more or less automatic—passive and partly involuntary —decisions of the writer.

---

[7] The humorist, Perelman, asked how he achieved such spontaneity in his writing joked—I paraphrase—that genuine spontaneity requires about 25 drafts. In a similar vein, Borges, for whom writing was an end in itself, quipped that the only reason to publish was to avoid endless revision.

The writer's decisions rely on concepts, language, imagery and *intentional* thought. Work is completed in stages as the individual returns again and again to potential for further composition.[8] The aim is to set down thoughts in words but the larger goal is completion of the work. Deliberation reflects choice or indecision, even if, unknown to and unfelt by the writer, the final selection is already decided. The animal's choices are immediate, more or less automatic but *purposeful*, depending on learning and drive. They do not evoke imagery so far as is known, but pertain to the momentary situation. Even an animal tracking a prey or a bird building a nest is not assumed to deliberate or have the final product or act in mind. A beaver does not, we presume, set out to build a dam, nor a spider a web. But the creative writer may also not know how his novel will end, or how to go from here to there. His efforts are concentrated on a brief phrase or idea in verbal imagery and focused, as Bosanquet wrote, on the keypad or the tip of his pen. We could say that intuition in the artist passes through an internal plane in thought that, unformed or inchoate, is the evolutionary outcome of instinct in the organism.

It may seem a stretch to compare drive behavior in animals to creative language in writers, but the animal generates behavior out of a virtual repertoire, partly innate, partly shaped by experience, as the writer taps phases of thought to effect verbal action based in imagery, derived from instinct and buried in the mental state. In the writer, a rich inventory of ideas and dispositions mediate, in recurrent volleys, a traversal from drive-potential to actual outcomes. Animal behavior is constrained by experience without imagery or evidence of deliberation. However, in both instances, behavior depends on learning, experience and skill, and arises out of tacit knowledge and memory. Even the themes of most novels—love, anger, hate, jealousy, ambition—are conceptual or affective derivations of the antecedent drives of hunger and sexuality (Brown,

---

[8] Most writers seek to recapture a mood or setting for each new attempt. Descartes wrote in bed, Samuel Johnson with a cat purring in his lap, Schiller with the smell of rotten apples in his desk. Much of my writing has been done near to water, the ocean, a pond or a pool.

2012). In sum, while there are enormous differences between animal behavior and human thought, there are important similarities that support a continuum theory of the creative act.

2. Creativity as a Continuum

To study creativity from the standpoint of genius, not as a general feature of mind except for adaptation, as in reconciling imagination and reality, excludes the problem from grades of creative activity, from animal cognition and evolutionary gradualism. The effect is to isolate study to infrequent examples of supremely gifted individuals, and the conditions that may contribute to their productivity. Most of these are extrinsic, such as family structure, childhood experience and education, or general features of the creative mind, such as personality and IQ. For some, only the final products are of significance, not the generative process. But the exegesis of a text or the analysis of a symphony rarely sheds light on how it was created, just as a thorough description of grammatical rules in dialogue or a game of chess does not clarify what goes on in the mind of an individual when he says a word or makes a move. Such external accounts can help to establish the uniqueness, quality and originality of a scientific or artistic product, and to rank the product according to a judgment of its worth, but they ignore the conceptions through which it actualizes, specifically, novelty in relation to recurrence in the process through which the actualization occurs.

Conversely, to argue for a continuum across evolutionary forms and from one mind to another runs the risk of diluting the concept to trivial examples of originality, whether unexpected behaviors, eccentric dress, cooking or clever remarks. A continuum from genius to ordinary cognition and from the latter to sub-human mind, barring a Rubicon at some stage in evolution or complexity, or the problematic concept of emergence, introduces the possibility of panpsychism, according to which creativity would be an inherent aspect of mentality that evolves to genius from intrinsic novelty in material nature. On this view, novelty in the highest grades represents the distal outcome of a natural process of creative transition. This implies that the metaphysics of change and the psychology of human creativity are realizations of a common process. While the distance in evolution or psychology from change in a basic entity to composition of the *Eroica* almost defies comprehension, and an exhaustive and probably controversial effort to identify intermediate stages is unlikely, there is no doubt that human mind evolved from animal mind and the latter from still more primitive organisms, indeed, from inanimate nature, so why not the same evolution for novelty? It is less likely that the evolutionary progression from the most elementary to the most complex required serial innovations *de novo* than that continuous permutations arise from an underlying pattern that is invisible precisely because it is uniform. Such an argument would be consistent with the belief expressed by William James that final explanation in psychology is metaphysical.

3. Gradations

In that a continuum entails an expansion over organisms and over millennia to genius from limited innovation or talent as a partial or weaker version, it is evident that certain properties of mind are common to all forms of creativity, as is their origin and relation to everyday thought. Given obvious differences of degree and kind, the relatedness is not as clear as the disparities. How should we compare Ravel to Beethoven? How are we to understand gradations from lesser to higher? How far down does the human continuum go, say from Beethoven through Ravel to Brecht to popular music and jingles? What do "degrees of genius" and differences in creative ability signify? Do different grades represent a fortuitous coming together of intelligence and experience with personality type; in other words, is genius an accident of nature and nurture? Staying with music as illustrative, to what extent does creativity apply to performance, as with a conductor or instrumentalist, where technique and interpretation rather than composition predominate? What are we to make of improvisation in jazz, which shows considerable invention but not on the order of a Haydn quartet? Does this pertain to the difference between originality and skill, repetition and innovation, creativity and talent?

With regard to talent, this represents the potential to learn a skill and the possibility of its creative use. Skill pertains to technique in the arts and method in the sciences, which are essential to the creation of novel products, though one can have the skill and create a work that is unoriginal, either by deficiency or accident. If someone solves a problem or composes a work of art, unaware of a prior example or discovery, as in the story *"Pierre Menand, Author of the Quixote"* by Borges, we might still attribute creativity to the effort, though the product would have no original scientific or artistic value. This differs from plagiarism or someone who copies a Vermeer to perfection. Clearly, there is skill but lack of originality. The series from an original to a fraud passes through skillful reproduction, both not uncommon in contemporary academics where historical memory is limited to a Google search. Indeed, amnesia or ignorance in the revival of prior work in various fields of science and psychology has made for many a successful career. This is no doubt more common in science than art, for the latter is more individualistic and recognizable.

Genius rests on skill, and encompasses and transcends talent. There is a recognition of higher and lower, or deeper and more superficial, grades of originality, even with an inability to account for the higher so as to exclude the lower, e.g. talent in performance and originality in composition, or within talent, the difference between, say, a highly skilled pianist and a rare virtuoso. A continuum entails an implicit process that extends from animal behavior to human thought, or a transition from earlier forms to capacities in higher mammals, e.g. dolphin, chimpanzee, and, I would claim, all the way down. There is no plausible alternative to a continuum that would not entail that genius and its approximations are exceptional developments of normal capacities but mutations —a gene complex, a "genius module"—not possessed by ordinary mortals. Such a "theory" could not account for lesser grades of creativity, the relation to ordinary cognition and evolutionary precursors. The problem is to identify the ground of novelty in the most primitive organisms, and their antecedents, and the foundational capacities out of which creativity develops. Given a continuum, what are these capacities?

Chapter 2

Preliminaries to a Theory of the Creative Process

Creative thought does not add, it empties.

The prerequisite for novelty in thought and behavior is an adaptive deviation from habit not indissolubly linked to sensibility. To some extent, the organism must adjust behavior to exigencies in the environment independent of habitual reactions and immediate sense data. To be ruled by sensibility leaves as little room for novelty as to be driven by routine or fixed instinct. The capacity for novel solutions to environmental conditions is characteristic of most species, at least down to reptiles and birds. The presumption is that novelty in behavior gradually internalizes to trial action or deliberation in thought and that this internalized phase underlies conceptual innovation. An evolutionary approach is critical, but variation, selection and adaptation are not sufficient to account for creativity, nor novelty in natural process. Yet, in that survival depends on adaptive strategies, it provides a mechanism for the most rudimentary innovations in the ancestral line.

Campbell (1960) and others (see Simontin, 1999) have argued for random variation and selection as a basis for creativity. Though some claim the importance of repression in the service of creativity, openness to a range of possibilities is characteristic of creative individuals as well as lower organisms. Fixed behavior dependent on habit and instinct are essential to survival in many species, and provide the basis for skill through learning, e.g. that colorful frogs give indigestion to predators. The elimination of a behavior by aversion is not fundamentally different from the discovery of a behavior or a gene through trial and error. In both, an advance in acts or concepts depends on constraints. The potential for deviation from routine, and the capacity for improvisation, are also necessary when fixed behavior is incompatible with a changing environment. The possibility of novel action can be taken to reflect the precedence of potential over commitment or a suspension of immediacy in the assertion of possibility.

Most organisms rely on a category of implicit responses, not an invariant repertoire triggered by the appropriate conditions. Since conditions — and, of necessity, responses — are not invariant, behavior must adapt to unexpected events in the ambient environment such as a shift in pattern or pattern recognition, varieties and degrees of threat, proximity of shelter, the same or different species, or defense of progeny. For the most part, evolutionary variation — random or otherwise — is a phenomenon relating to population, not cognitive, diversity. In animals, the apparent absence of an inner life reinforces the impression of reflex-like behavior. However, the potential for diverse behaviors — spontaneous, discovered or curtailed by learning — is most likely a precursor of human categories that incorporate the possibility of a multitude of outcomes, all of which — tacit or virtual — are unrealized prior to final specification.

Confidence and inventiveness in creative individuals gives an expectation of some form of novelty but not the content of the novel product. Uncertainty gives greater surprise, with deviation in arousal from a potential that tends to specify established routes of development. A departure from the habitual occurs mainly at segments midway between the relative fixity of instinct and apparent mind-independence of causal passage, just as in evolution novel forms arise from pre-terminal stages.[9] What begins as impulse or disposition and ends in adaptive behavior undergoes a branching — derailment, propagation — by way of verbal or visual imagery. Some operations of the dream work are involved — condensation, fusion, displacement, etc. — but unlike dream, which lacks a veridical endpoint, creative thought, however fantastic, must ultimately, if it is to be understood and appreciated, adapt to the physical and social environment. The image(s) selected may reflect subtle bias at different points in the derailment; the motif, the idea, what is aroused, what is discarded. Serial derivations from idea to product can be described as probabilistic but not random, since the outcome is subject to the constraints of the idea and its revival over successive states. The account of deviation, e.g. metaphor and other whole/part relations, in terms of probabilities fits with the experience of creative individuals who "discover" their own thoughts in the course of thinking, as well as the feeling of passivity or receptiveness to emerging ideas, since originality is not forecast in prior states or obligated by baseline conditions.

1. Novelty and Sensibility

Let us return to the observation that the inner, as the source of creativity, exhibits relative constancy in spite of the flux of mental content, while the outer, though of a deep uniform fabric, is ever and never the same. Novelty in perceptual nature — incessant change in the observed world and the sensibility to which mind adapts — is not understood in the same way as creativity in human mind. The appearance of novel states-of-affairs in the world might reflect a creative process in nature, and creativity in nature may well be the foundation of creativity in thought, but sensibility, though essential for knowledge of the world, is antithetical in some respects to human creativity. Indeed, after a period of learning and study, and saturation with the world, it is likely, in most creative individuals, that an attraction to the world and a dependence

---

9   For the role of neoteny and parcellation in novel thought and evolutionary advance, see Brown (2010; 2015).

on sensation must be in abeyance to liberate the internal process of genuine creativity. If there is creativity in mind-independent nature, one source would be uni-directional growth in the evolution of the organic world (Bergson, 1911), which can be interpreted as non-random and as having a subjective aim (Whitehead, 1933), though not necessarily subject to a guiding mentality.

Successive states of becoming in the natural world actualize over their precedents out of a potential for recurrence. The epoch develops over its immediate ancestor prior to completion and prior to perishing. Even with instinctual drive at one pole and an assault by sensation at the other, mind creates novel objects, as in the beaver's dam, a novel structure in its own right but one that forms new lakes and habitats. Change in the world induced by the human mind is essentially limitless, from the steam engine to blowing up the planet. Mind can change the world and the world changes mind or contributes to novelty as the "raw data" out of which the creative is elaborated.

The distinction of novelty and repetition, or innovation and habit, is a central problem for causal theory as well as for recurrence models, such as microgenesis, or for related concepts such as Buddhism, which postulate an iteration of momentary states (epochs) in contrast to an open-ended concatenation or box-car chain of causal events. Novelty in thought is intrinsic; it can remain implicit in successive epochs or expand in consciousness to novel concepts. Sensibility contributes to constant change, but it is only one side of novelty, suppressing images that are not useful or adaptive. In human mind, novelty in recurrence contrasts with a repetition occasioned by fixed instinct and minimal change in sensibility across adjacent epochs. In human mind, a reduction of the influence of sensation is essential to creative thinking. Take for example the common experience of lying awake in bed at night, eyes closed, sensation at a minimum, while a stream of novel images passes through the mind. A relative freedom from sensation relaxes constraints on thought allowing novel ideas to surface that would otherwise be aborted by sensory necessity. Wordsworth's recollection in tranquility comes to mind.

In the case of human creativity, there is an inverse relation to sensibility. Once knowledge is ingrained through sensory contact with the world, with sufficient experience and skill, when there is a relaxation of immediate sensation through withdrawal, isolation, an inward turn, or when the endogenous overrides sensory adaptation, the individual will be inattentive to external stimuli. At this point, mind-internal can undergo exploration and the coming-to-the-fore of images that would otherwise be parsed by sensation. Such images can be creative and lead to original works or they can remain fantasies, visions, hallucinations, at times highly original but without significance for unique discovery. This is why creative imagery in dream occurs when sensory constraints on thought are attenuated and the inner life takes precedence.

The sensory world, in change and stability, is responsible for the relative sameness of succession and the relative novelty across moments. Unlike mind, change in physical passage is not conceptual, though one can speak of prior-categories. In human mind, proximal phases in the mind/brain state (the self, experience, character) show minimal change across epochs, while distal or "world-close" segments (speech, perception) show emphatic change. Stasis is concealed change or unobservable novelty. There is no unchanging persistence. Stability across states owes to the overlap of similar epochs, to the gradual nature of change in the world and to the sculpting of maladaptive possibilities. Even habit shows a grain of novelty, minimally in the accretion of behaviors by way of reinforcement. A world of constant change, e.g. in object size, shape, motion or location, contrasts with the apparent persistence, lawfulness and predictability of the world as a whole. The laws of physical nature are reliable; they are not suspended for novelty, which either does not exist, i.e. is a causal outcome, or is a hidden feature of natural law, even if the diversity of instantiations is ascribed to probability and contingency.

The locality of object change is embedded in the stability of recurrence on a grander scale. Sensation can evoke a simulacrum of novelty in mind, for example, an unfamiliar face or encounter; in the world, an earthquake. We believe each moment is different from the last though we conceive novelty, in the sense of a departure from causal certainty, as intermittent and contingent, and ultimately explicable on the basis of physical law. On this view, non-causal novelty is like a miracle, a violation of natural law. Given the difficulties with genuine novelty in a world of universal causation, it is understandable that theory on this topic is guided more by deference to classical physics than the relation of mind to sensibility.

A perception provokes a novel idea when it releases (disinhibits) an image by the suppression of virtual competitors. In the succession of world-states, change in passage also brings change in sensibility. *Novelty in the changing appearances of the world is in the formative process through which objects develop. Perceptions are not the birthing of cognitions but their goal.* Every perception conceals a process of creation that is overcome by the sensibility it seeks to realize. In a word, the novelty of entities in the world is trivially represented by change in passage, while the genuine novelty in physical entities and perceptual objects is buried in the finality of object form, surfacing as imagery when that finality is incomplete. Relative freedom from the external is necessary for the expansion of novelty to a creative idea. Sensation carves out intrinsic knowledge; it does not instill experience but works through the delimitation of possibility. The source of experience is a sensibility that carves possibility into particulars. As the linguist Roman Jacobson noted, babbling in the infant progresses from a potential for producing the speech sounds of all natural languages to those of the mother tongue. The sculpting of language by sensibility results in the elimination of maladaptive trends, in this instance, sounds that do not fit with those in the linguistic environment of the infant. This puts into figural prominence features of language and perception that mirror a personal model of reality. For most, thought is habitual cognition sculpted by sense data to fit, not invent, an extra-personal world. The real is inimical to the creative. Sensation parses fantasy and blocks all but what is immediately relevant, while creativity requires a departure from the given.

In this respect, creativity is adulterated by convention. As Kant put it, taste clips the wings of genius.

The outcome of this line of thought is a view of creativity in which a continuum of novelty is ingredient in psychic process and nature. Novelty in passage is expanded to the creativity of thought. Novelty is continuous and ubiquitous, since intermittent novelty would violate natural law, while the creative, though founded on novelty, is an intermittent accentuation of novelty. The idea that the process of nature exhibits genuine novelty in every occasion of change runs up against universal causation, which entails that change is causally determined and genuine novelty impossible. The assumption here is that the *psychology of human creativity, as an occasion of emphasis, is bound to the passage of nature in a metaphysics of novel change.*

2. Iteration and Deviation

A central property of an original act and the crux of creative thought is deviation from habit or expectancy. This could be construed as a failure of repetition since each recurrence is minimally novel in comparison to its antecedents, in part due to changing sensibility, in part to fluctuations in the resting state. Incessant change is resolved with continuity in the revival of mental states, in the growth of private experience and the passage of objects in the world. The continuity resolves the sameness of things with novelty in their recurrence. Whether a thing changes rapidly — a film, an argument — or slowly — the self, a rock — transition over moments is continuous. The paradox is that in spite of continuity, things exist as modular epochs of becoming with no gaps in experience or perceptible nature.[10] Things recur and each recurrence is novel though retaining ingredients of the prior epoch. The difference between exact iteration, novelty in passage and fresh renewal depends on more than a difference in succession since a world in continuous change is the main source of the disparity, and a self of moderate stability is the arbiter of sameness and difference.

---

[10]   Even across sleep or loss of consciousness there is felt continuity of the self.

In this context it is important to emphasize again that genuine change occurs in the actualization of an epoch and that apparent or illusory change occurs in the transition of one epoch to another. Genuine change is the becoming-into-being (existence) of an entity—the actualization of a sequence of categories—while apparent change is the progression from one epoch of being to another, namely, the observed and presumed causal sequence of events in the world. An epochal state is an instance of being that is inert, its dynamic—becoming— exhausted in its formation. The process of entity creation is complete on the actualization of an epoch of being (category, substance), which on achieving existence passes away in its replacement, while continuity depends on the overlap of epochs (Fig. 2.1).

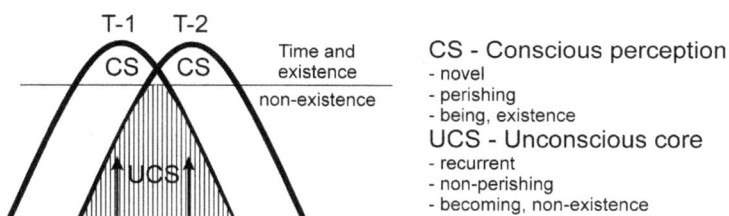

Fig. 2.1: Phases in working memory are generally revived in ensuing states in the order of their registration, i.e. in relation to their resemblance to the oncoming state and, thus, their capacity for revival. Images closer to the current perception, i.e. those in short-term memory that almost achieve re-perception, are most likely to be revived in the current state. The mind/brain state at T-1 is replaced by an overlapping state at T-2. The core of T-1 is overlapped at T-2 before T-1 terminates, i.e. before the epoch exists. This explains the recurrence of early phases in T-1 associated with individuality, self, character, dispositions, long-term and experiential memory, and the "persistence" of core beliefs, values and personality. Later phases perish on completion of the entire state to make way for novel perceptions. The reactivation of earlier phases by the overlapping state explains the sustained personhood behind succession. Early phases are ingredient across states, later ones are malleable to a greater extent as endogenous process is shaped by sensation.

We perceive events, not objects. An event is the more or less arbitrary duration over a series of recurrent epochs. The rate of replacement is probably constant for each entity, while event-duration, which depends on the limits of an event, can be rapid (a punch) or slow (a prizefight). The change is attributed to a changing or transitory object, i.e. to objects or events in the world, whereas genuine change in the observer's mind is imperceptible.

Ideas come and go, but mind-internal seems much the same from one moment to the next. There is no definite feeling of a forward motion or advance. One can think about the future but not have the feeling of a movement toward it, as one can think about the past without a sense of time-reversal or return. In contrast, the outer aspect of mind — the perceptual world — moves in a forward direction. The self as a center of experience imagines a future to which it and the world are inexorably striving, but it is the world, or the external aspect of mind, that has a forward direction. The internal aspect, for which the future is an idea, may be tinged with dread or anticipation, but the inner life is restricted to the now. Expectation concerns the possibility that some idea or condition will occupy a future present. Expectancy touches a feeling of the inescapability of forward passage.

Accordingly, the depth of self in memory and its role in the creation of the present give the feeling of transition from *past to present*, which differs from external perception, which has a direction from *present to future*, with the combination account-ing for the sense of causal progression. Though firmly fixed in the present, self or thought may be felt as an inclination to the future or an impulse to a further point. One could say the self has one foot in the past of memory and another in the present of perception, while perception has one foot in the passing present and another in the immediate future. Many forms of imagery take the self into the past. Perception carries the self into the future. Though transition appears continuous, a suspension of perceptual experience, in dream or sensory deprivation, accompanies a reduction in the feeling of forward advance. One cannot catch a perception, Hume wrote. Every perception has a quality of futurity. In the continuous transition of objects, perception is conceived as external and objective, while the present, generated by the self and forming its perspective, is the ground of subjectivity. There is a balance between stasis and advance, between the presentness of the subjective and the forward surge of the objective. A focus of consciousness on memory and the past will be accompanied by inwardness and retreat, while a shift in focus to changing sensibility carries attention into the future. In this way the relative stability of personal continuity is resolved with the freshness of perceptual renewal.

Depth and surface in the mind/brain state, though metaphors for the relation of past to present, whole to part, earlier to later, before to after, mind to world, onset to terminus, ancient to recent, unconscious to conscious, are apt depictions of an epochal state of human mind, in relation to which transition in the physical entities of mind-independent nature is rudimentary. Since nature is interpreted through the filter of human mentality, the pattern of actualization in mind serves as a model for the material world, or at least one can, in principle, extend some features of the actualization of the mind/brain state to physical entities. This strategy differs from the usual approach in that it traces a relatively mature theory of human mind (microgenesis) back through its evolutionary history to simple organisms, even material entities, presuming that some features of the higher will appear in the lower. This is in contrast to beginning with genes and physics and collating basic units to increasingly higher forms, a strategy used to justify the disassembly and reconstitution of complex systems.

In this respect, some features of the mind/brain state that are presumably common to physical entities are becoming-into-being, the epochal nature of things, and the problem of continuity and atomicity. In this mix, the whole/part relation is universal, interpreted as the whole of an epoch that enfolds the parts (phases) of its becoming, or the whole of the onset of the epoch in relation to the particulars that emerge on completion. This is less clear in a basic entity such as a particle than in a primitive organism. But if every entity recurs over its own "structure" and vanishes into the past on completing one cycle of existence, how do we account for the recurrence of the "same" entity? If one epoch of a thing becomes past, thus non-existent, as the next epoch takes its place, how is the initial epoch preserved in its successor? Where does the successor come from and how does it retain features of its antecedents (see Fig. 2.1).

The problem is no less difficult for a particle than a mental state, though with the latter one has to contend with "societies" of physical and organic elements — for example, a neuron (itself a society), the person as a whole and the perceptual world. The membranous boundary of a nerve cell, as well as its infrastructure, is indistinct from the context, connectivity and chemistry of brain tissue. The neuron is a whole to its constituents and a part to the rest of the brain, as the brain is a constituent of a person, and the person is a locus in space-time. Every occasion is a matter of scale, from a superstring to a galaxy. Things recur at different rates. The mind/brain has a rate of recurrence that incorporates an enormous multiplicity of elements, each with its own rate of replication. The developing mental state entrains these elements such that, one might suppose, the final epoch realizes a unity of its constituents, and the constituents subserve the unity of the actual state.

For Whitehead, unity is achieved by feeling (prehensions), not an unlikely possibility (Chapter 12). The question is whether a "society", small or large, comes together in an act of becoming to recur as a novel whole, or whether the recurrence and partition of a given occasion enfolds different rates in the replacement of constituent elements. The rates of recurrence of the innumerable constituents of a mind/brain state would be a fraction of the state as a whole. This raises the question, how to reconcile variable rate of recurrence, or the duration and becoming of myriad epochs, with the larger whole in which they are embedded? Clearly, there are difficulties in a recurrence theory, but comparable problems bedevil causation, such as relation of part to whole, atomicity and change and, especially, the preservation of the cause in the effect.

Chapter 3

Causation
A Problematic Theory

The deepest questions have no answers.

The concept of causation does not allow for genuine novelty, even though the effect differs from the cause and in this respect is novel. The transition to effect is assumed to be fully given in the cause, even if what is given, and the "givenness", cannot be specified. Except for such instances as billiard ball causation, in which objects are much the same except for motion and energy transfer, causal relations are generally unable to illuminate— nor can one enumerate— the exact ingredients of change in the causal step. A simple motor reflex with two neurons still involves cell membranes, axonal transport, neurotransmitters, the synaptic environment, refractoriness, excitatory and inhibitory potentials, and so on (Hebb, 1949). There is nothing simple about it. What exactly is the cause of a movement: an act of will, an axonal impulse, synaptic events, receptor surface? Even a complete description of the cause would not satisfy the transition to an effect, since the cause itself will change on its description, i.e. there are no unchanging things. A similar description of the effect is no more helpful, in part because the cause no longer exists at the instant of the effect, and the change in transition is not satisfied by an account of the outcome. The inability to capture change differs from the problem of position and velocity, in that velocity is rate of change, not change, and position is always changing. For this reason, change is conceived as a succession of states, each depicted as cause or effect without interval.

On this view, cause and effect have an object-like character, in that their description and the transition from cause to effect, however dynamic, are necessarily static once described. This transition, though presumed to incorporate the prior state, decomposes to subsets of changing states or objects. An account of the *relata* in a causal pair as terms, facts, events, etc. is an objectification of change. The attempt to overcome the elusiveness of actual change through measurement replaces an observation of invisible process with a calculus of energy and/or velocity. This shifts actual change over an event to a rate or trajectory, or a comparison of a thing at one time to the same or different thing at another time.

In a spinal reflex, one can say that striking the patellar tendon sends a signal to the spinal cord, which results in a motor discharge, muscle contraction and a jerk of the leg. The intermediary steps can be studied in some detail but it comes down to this: A goes to B, such that A does something to induce B. B can be another object or event—a billiard ball or muscle contraction—or B can be a new state of A. In the former case, one has a micro-depiction of embedded causal pairs, say membrane chemistry—certainly a significant achievement— but, even at this "simple" level, the *relata* in each pair, though describable, are interpreted in terms of energy transfer while the change across *relata* eludes description. The transition from a just-before to a just-after embraces a series of intercalated steps, each capable of further decomposition, ultimately to an atomic or molecular basis. Each causal pair encloses or can be reduced to a microscopic series of pairs at a lower level of description—in fact, a near-infinite regress within the transition —leaving the actual change from cause to effect opaque. Though change in causal transition evades description, it is assumed to be determined by properties of the cause. When novel or unforeseen outcomes appear, especially in complex systems, they are presumed to be resultants from events yet-to-be-described. In a word, causation assumes certainty of outcome, or theoretical predictability, even if all the data needed to calculate the effect are not available, when in fact the very grounds of a prediction of effect from cause are uncertain.

One can say that while causation is assumed prior to its demonstration, causal theory is conceived as universally valid and anterior to explanation in physical and organic systems. This follows from its relevance to logic, from successful application to physical science, and the invariance of physical law, while the stages in a causal step, often beyond the known properties of the immediate object, are presumed efficacious even if unobservable. If A changes into B, what precisely transpires? Alternatively, consider an object in change, whether stationary or moving. In a continuous motion, such as a bird in flight or an athlete in competition, even when the series is filmed in slow motion and the continuity of the action is measured in detail, a sequence of static frames in close association still does not reveal the transfer of characteristics over states, just the difference in the frames. Causation, which is a theory of change, cannot give a convincing response to the objections that have been raised, and yet others below, nor can it give an account of the very process it claims to explain.

This is also the case with the *sequence of mind/brain states* that generate an action. The mind/brain state is the proximate cause of the act, but it is not possible to identify the multiplicity of cells, networks and patterns that have a direct impact. The mind/brain state behind observable behavior is inscrutable. Yet, as Hume argued, mind contributes causal power to the transmission across contiguous objects. Though not observable, causal interaction in brain is inferred from behavior. In contrast, macroscopic events in behavior and in the world are observable, but judged to conform to logical, not physical, necessity. This implies that a theory of physical causation has its roots in the feeling of agency, and that causal logic precedes physical causation.

Given the mind-dependence of causal necessity, a willful randomness of action can defy explanation on a causal basis. If I say "chair", then "Venezuela", then "oobie-doobie", then gurgle, in rapid succession, it is supposed there are associative links from one state to another, and an imaginative observer could likely find some connection, but stages in succession, which constitute the microtransition of events, can never be precisely elucidated. The need for coherence or meaning in a sequence of events reinforces the interpretation of such events in terms of causal logic, while an illogical sequence, whether or not deliberate, affirms the priority of logical relations over genuine causation, since it is presumed that any sequence must be caused even if it is irrational. This disconnect in logical and illogical sequences — or their correlates in brain — poses a considerable problem for causal theory, for it illustrates that causal logic, which itself begins with a primitive feeling of agency,[11] is prior to the physical causation on which it is subsequently modeled. This provides yet another argument for the mind-dependence of our notion of causal necessity.

As noted, if change is continuous one could, in principle, slice transition at any point, say between A and B. This entails a regress of points or degrees of change in a causal pair, a dilemma avoided if change is construed as simultaneous. But if so, how and when does the transformative step occur? If change from A to B is simultaneous, so is that from A to G, since the simultaneity from A to B will apply to that from B to C, C to D and so on. If one transition is simultaneous, so are all transitions and causal passage unfolds like a film from a movie reel. This is not inconceivable, at least theoretically, and it is consistent with the transition from the simultaneity of the unconscious to the temporal order of conscious experience, but it does violence to common sense, not to mention the whole of scientific and psychological explanation. In that simultaneity of cause and effect entails an absence of transition, it is a finesse that excludes change without clarifying it. On the other hand, if a sequence is not simultaneous and its stages cannot be specified, causation is a theory by default.

How is something changed to something else? This usually presumes that the same thing changes, not that each change results in a new thing. A bird in flight is the same bird that was perched on a branch a moment before. Change is conceived as adventitious to identity. A person changes every moment but is inferred to be the same person over the change. It is only when changed things are compared over a longer duration or when

---

[11]   See commentary on Guyau in Michon et al. (1988). Many theorists have argued the animistic or anthropomorphic roots of agency.

change is dramatic that we say the change results in a changed object (person) or that the object is no longer the same. Sameness and difference are bound up with the concept of identity. This requires more discussion, but in brief, identity is a subjective judgment that depends on the categorical nature of objects.

With respect to brain activity, the cause or causal complex of a given state of brain is left undetermined, as is the way an effect comes about. The before and after of the millions of cells and connections that are engaged in the simplest act are of such nuance and complexity as to make a precise and complete specification of the cause impossible. Indeed, the circuit-board diagrams of cognitive studies would be ludicrous if they were not taken seriously. The output of a series is presumed to be the terminus of a causal chain with the sequence conceived as a transfer of information from one entity to another. This collapses change to a connection between hypothetical entities, and leaves unanswered every pertinent question concerning causal relations. The account of entities with an output that passes information from one object to another implies that change involves substantives, e.g. "bits", or that change can be described in object-like terms.

A further problem concerns the absorption of the cause into the effect and its loss in the past when the effect comes about. If the effect does not absorb the complete cause, and the cause, once lost, is lost forever, the loss of information once the cause no longer exists leaves every effect to some extent dissociated from its antecedents. All that survives is the effect, which immediately vanishes into the next state. All that existed in the past, the before of transition or physical passage, is now part of the passing effect, the after, isolated from its ancestry and passing on those features of the cause instrumental in its induction. In organic systems, especially human mind, this problem is mitigated by memory, where much that is remembered, and much that is not, is revived in the present. But how memory is recovered in transition, and how the past continues into the present, is a complex problem that is a critical aspect of temporal passage, not only in human mind but in physical nature as well.

The account of mental functions as interactive solids is especially vulnerable to the onset of an ensuing sequence. If I say the word "chair", does the word or act, or its neural correlate, serve as a causal link for the one that follows, i.e. is the effect the cause of another effect, particularly in a repetition of the same or similar word or act? Or does the act vanish as other causal sequences come into play? If the final output vanishes so the sequence can be repeated, the break in causation argues against chain theory and supports a recurrence model.

Take a mind/brain state that eventuates in an act, an object or a word. The object is conceived as causal input to the brain, while a word or act is its causal output. To assume a causal chain that begins with an object or ends with a word, apart from problems noted thus far, begs the question of the selection of the item, its context, fate and precursors, leaving aside the problem of object perception which has been discussed *in extenso* elsewhere. A word is generally a response (command, question) to an interlocutor and is meant to have a particular effect; thus its cause can be said to be partly external. The inferred knowledge of another mind plays a causal role in word selection. What then of the ensuing word, its spontaneity or voluntary character, its grammatical relation to other words, immediate, prior or forthcoming, the force and intention of the word, not to mention its meaning, phonology and articulation? What is the causal role of bypassed and/or covert stages in the A to G of word production, if one does not assume a strictly contained reflex-like sequence that aims at and terminates in the final word?

Presumably, the process of word-production begins with core process, or the kernel of the utterance, leads through object and lexical concepts to phonological segments that excite the articulators, a sequence that pertains more to the logic of word production than to the neural carriers of the transitional sequence. Unless A is the sole cause of B without remainder, and B the sole cause of C, each stage in a causal chain will have multiple immediate and secondary effects, and each effect other than B or C will have its own causal consequences. At some point, the end of a causal sequence is reached, but how can one distinguish the endpoint — its selection, timing, fate — from the innumerable "side-effects" or branches of the chain? What impels the selection of a word is not just its category-relations. If I can produce a nonsense word, an unexpected word or one in another language, along with what is not produced as a concomitant or antecedent, how can we ever determine proximate cause?

Moreover, if causation is continuous, it is endless and there is no break or endpoint in a chain. How do we mark off events as complete and distinct from ensuing events? When a moving object becomes stationary, we assume the event is over, but the object persists and change is going on. The bird that lands on a branch continues to live, to move, to perceive, to change. Whether the event duration is a lengthy flight or a brief perch, what constitutes an event is an arbitrary span in the mind. The upshot of this line of thought is that events are categories demarcated in the mind.

Ordinarily, we think of causation as an open-ended succession, but the process that has been discussed — word-production — involves a sequence of phases that are traversed in every act of cognition. The iteration of the same phases — object-concept, lexical-semantics, phonology — is essential to each occasion of speech. The problem is the same for the psychology of generative grammar, in that an utterance is the surface outcome of an unconscious onset, e.g. topic-action. This iteration is not dissimilar, in principle, to object-persistence. The problem of the origination of successive mental states is comparable to that of the recurrence of an object, a person, which can be cause or effect of some event, but also a cause to its own persistence. Many writers, such as Lewis (1986), reduce the problem of causal persistence to that of causal parts, consistent with the mereological concept of wholes as containers. This philosopher does ask "must an adequate understanding make no reference to unactualized possibilities?", but he does not pursue the question.

This raises a central problem: namely, if the endpoint of a causal series is the cause of an ensuing series, what instigates the subsequent state? Every state requires a "first mover." Thus, if A is essential to the production of G, once G occurs, how on the basis of causal theory does the process revert to A? The word at G requires a sequence of stages in its production. Once the word is produced it is past. How does the final effect of the chain evoke the initial stage (A) for the sequence to recur, not only for words but for all acts or outputs? A causal sequence leading to an output cannot avoid a causal account of a similar state with a similar outcome. In the absence of such an account, there is an explanatory gap for events that begin a causal series, as well as those intermediate between onset and termination, and consequent to the terminus. Postulating a trigger or pacemaker for the onset of a state, though plausible, is inconsistent with a causal account. Yet in spite of such problems, causation remains the primary, if not sole, scientific theory of change.

Consider these problems from another perspective. If the neural substrate that corresponds to a word is the cause of a subsequent effect, what is the status of events that are peripheral to the primary series? How does the incitement of a novel series occur when the prior one is complete? It would seem improbable for a word, as the finality of a causal chain, to serve, in the speaker, as an intermediate step in the arousal of an ensuing state. There cannot be an open-ended concatenation of every outcome if comparable sequences are to arise.

Leaving aside these difficulties and the necessity for recurrence, which is inexplicable on causal chain theory, if we grant that change is continuous, and causal, there is the problem of the freedom to elicit a novel occasion from causal imperatives in every state or constituent. A refusal to act is a veto at the conscious endpoint, but can the self block or alter a process that is largely unconscious? The fact that the major part of the cognitive process is unconscious, and unalterable by conscious effort, does not mean it is automatic or causal, since novel change, and creativity in general, are outcomes of unconscious transition.

Similarly, an intention, which is itself an act, should logically precede the act intended, but it is unclear, from work such as that of Libet (1985), how the intention once initiated affects the outcome. Clearly, there is a degree of freedom within the actualization process, thus an escape from causal determinism, since creativity is unconscious. This raises the prickly question of freedom in relation to novelty as unconscious deviation from expectation. We tend to think that true freedom is an intentional act in defiance of causal inevitability, though it could be maintained that the intervention of an intentional state is itself an accompaniment or causal interlude in an unconscious chain. Without such intervention, causation — soft or hard (Laplacean) — leads to a mechanical or robotic determinism that is independent of the actor's desires and inconsistent with inherent novelty or intermittent creativity.

Novelty as an emergent would be an occasional, not intrinsic, property of change. The idea that novelty occurs only in systems in a particular state of complexity implies intermittency, but sheds no light on underlying process. As an emergent, novelty could be explained on a causal basis as the product of covert resultants, but how would a string of resultants explain a great work of art, especially if the work is conceived, even visualized, as a whole, such that its constituents occur simultaneously with the causal sequence of composition illusory? In complex systems, novelty could be probabilistic and still causal, but how do causal and largely unconscious probabilities lead to an integrated and meaning-laden product, a novel or symphony, recursion, a theme and variations, or melodies that span individual tones? The implication that novelty is episodic, like creativity, conflicts with the account here proposed, in which genuine novelty is inherent, independent of complexity and a foundational property of brain process. A genuine novelty that is inherent in change is essential if blind chance and causal necessity are to be rescued from incoherence.

A fundamental error in applying causal thinking to cognition is the extension of relations between logical solids to those involving the organic substrates on which the logic supervenes. As to the constituents of an act of cognition, various components are isolated, de-contextualized and treated as independent, demarcated entities. However, a lexical-category or object-concept provides a contextual background out of which a word or object arises, a background that is largely eliminated if the item is conceived as a bounded solid

articulated by an equally non-contextual phonological key-
board or a perceptual assembly apparatus. What stands behind
a word or object, its experiential relations, identity, meaning,
import, i.e. its unconscious infrastructure, cannot be dissociated
from the actuality to which it leads. Just as a perceptual object is
embedded in the world, or the world is revived with the object
as a figural prominence, a word arises as a verbal act out of
personal experience, vocabulary, intent and functional role.

The series leading to a perception or the transition to
articulation, though referred to the brain, is a logical sequence
of steps in the construction or elicitation of the item. It is presumed that the progression from one logical entity to another is
mirrored in the brain, with the final event—word, object—
conceived as an output of a causal series, not as is the case, a
mind/brain state that embodies all phases in its realization.
Specifically, the meaning, intent or purpose, and experience
that are ingredient in an act of cognition, as well as possible
lines of development that are aroused but unrealized, are not
left behind as past phases, or rejected alternatives, as would
occur in a causal model, but persist with the final word or
object as part of the epochal state.

The discussed inadequacies of causal theory, especially in
its application to brain and organism, are precisely the
strengths of microgenesis, in that every state has a new
beginning, every terminus perishes as another state re-boots,
and outcomes incorporate, but are not the irrevocable effects of,
their predecessors. Within a state, antecedent contents are
potentials or probabilities, not inevitabilities. Across states,
what survive are the initial segments constrained by the preceding state. The proximal (earlier) phases may well have
causal relations to their antecedents, i.e. the overlay of early
segments, while the distal (later) phases appear relatively stable
through the influence of external constraints (sensibility), habit
and the impact of antecedent segments. Distal objectivities—
the finalities of the subjective or extra-personal aim—traverse
intermediate segments of imagery which—whether latent or
manifest—have a greater capacity for deviation from occurrent
and ancestral patterns. Causal relations may well figure in the
processing sequence, but as incidental to qualitative

transformation. The shift from whole to part at any phase in the epoch might be a function of probabilities that follow causal laws, but the elicitation of category-members is parsed by constraints, not urged onward by necessity.

Put otherwise, phases in the mind/brain state are not impelled by posterior cause but survive a suppression of alternatives. Constraints on virtual members constitute a filter for a selection that allows targets to emerge, but not as a direct cause of the partition. The specification of parts from wholes, or items from categories, occurs at every phase, not as causal resultants but as the residue of what is left after other possibilities are eliminated. These bypassed or unrealized alternatives provide a context that is incorporated with the final epoch. The sequence that lays down the mind/brain state does not eventuate in a causal output but fills a duration from onset to terminus — non-temporal until complete — such that the final actuality enfolds all phases in its realization.

Chapter 4

Process Theory

Truth, like gold, is obtained...
by washing away all that is not gold.
— Leo Tolstoy

1. The Contrast with Causation

The preceding discussion introduced the microgenetic concept in relation to the mind/brain state and its inferred application to organism and physical entity. The process account resolves problems of continuity and change that are not adequately addressed in causal theory. The central point is that a brain state is an epoch that begins to recur before it fully becomes what it is, or achieves an epoch of existence.[12] The significance of overlap is that the onset of an epoch — a mental state, an entity — is retraced by the oncoming epoch before the present one terminates, such that the preliminary is replaced before the state achieves actuality. An actualization that does not complete one cycle of being does not achieve existence. The revival of early phases, in preserving core attributes of the prior state, including personality, character, foundational beliefs and values, provides continuity in the depth of epochal structure (Fig. 2.1). The self remains much the same, while the world is in constant change. The penultimate phase of microgenesis, with a relaxation of sensibility and a distance from drive, has the capacity for conceptual growth and creative departure from

---

[12]   William James appears have been the first to emphasize the overlap of successive states but he did not explore the full significance of this insight.

inner (instinctual drive) and outer (sensory-determined) outcomes.

In human mind, early phases of overlap show relative stability in transition in the face of continuous change in perception. An intermediate level in thought prior to an objective endpoint is the ostensible engine of creativity, though multiple phases in every act of thought display novelty and the capacity for displacement to novelty. Incompleteness in revival, interpreted as decay or forgetting, occur top-down as a recession from the endpoint. The replication of the preliminary and constraints on the terminus are such that it is primarily the intermediate segments of tacit or manifest imagery that are capable of divergence from the directives of instinctual drive, the compulsions of habit and the obligations of sensibility.

It is counter-intuitive but nonetheless true that, from an internalist perspective, objects in perception are lifeless markers of the dynamic of their creation. Becoming deposits entities that die the moment of their birth. The process of creation in mind-external — the procession of inert, perishing forms, organic and inanimate — is obscured by the rapid replacement that gives the illusion of external change. However, change, and with it novelty, occurs *within* an epoch over a brief series that is relatively identical to its antecedents, though a longer series gives the impression of more noticeable change. A person appears much the same over minutes or hours but not years. A rock appears the same over years, but over a sufficient duration, the change would be apparent, depending on conditions.

As discussed, continuity is guaranteed by the overlap of contiguous epochs, i.e. the initiation of T-2 before the actuality of T-1. In human mind, early phases concurrent with the self and experiential history preserve identity across temporally continuous states. The overlap of contiguous states, or rather, the absorption of one state into another, gives a seamless transition. The difference or lack of sameness in mental content is magnified at later phases when that which is endogenous in human mind, relatively free from drive at its origin and the effects of sensibility at the terminus, can undergo a novelty that, when magnified, becomes creative thought. The perceptual model at the world surface of mind — the endpoint of the state—appears and disappears in each recurrence. This is less an erasure or rapid forgetting than a perishing of the epoch with preservation of the preliminary in the replacement, which is well on the road to actuality. The concept of forgetting as incomplete revival, not trace decay, has been discussed in prior works.

This differs from a succession of modular units—point-instants in Buddhist metaphysics—linked together by causal relations. In Buddhist theory, point-instants arise, abide and perish, but in microgenetic theory there is no abidance, which is another term for persistence. Whether object- or event-causation, whether local or generalized, imminent or indirect, the causal chain, however complex and uncertain, would go, in principle, from (final) effect to further cause, with events linked together of arbitrary duration, such that the endpoint of an event is the cause of another event, no matter how final the earlier event appears to be, or how vague or deviant the event that ensues. Even the finality of death is the cause of a series of events—metabolic, parasitic, entropic, historical, social—that lead to a further series of outcomes. But what of those final events that terminate and give way to a repetition of the same or similar sequence, as in the song of a nightingale that, once over, begins again? How does the last tone of the song cause the first tone of its repetition? In the idea of replication of successive epochs, microgenesis resolves the causal gap from the endpoint of one sequence to the onset of the next.

In a causal chain, the cause no longer exists, or is a memory, at the instant of the effect, while the effect belongs to a non-existent future at the instant of the cause. Even if the transmission from cause to effect is simultaneous, as some have proposed, there would have to be transitional states within a causal pair, in fact an infinite regress of such states, a difficulty that traces back to Zeno.[13] Process theory makes this problem tractable in the idea of overlapping epochs and a recurrence theory of change. Things seem to move to the future, but the loss of one instance of being, not its death or eradication but its

---

[13]   See discussion in Emmet (1985).

absorption into the past, fails to explain the occurrence of the next. If passage is a knife-edge in the transition of before to after, from no-longer to not-yet, an actuality will appear, re-appear and pass away.

The arising of an act or object out of drive and the imagination is modulated by a downstream sensibility that adapts mind to world and maintains the continuity of inner and outer with minimal transformation, even though phases in experiential memory contribute to the individual character of a mental state. The specificity and meaning of an object, its uniqueness in time, place and personal signification, reflect passage through such phases. In this process, the inner life undergoes incessant change, usually modest, at times dramatic, but the relative constancy of the self as a recurrent center of experience lends stability to what can either be a logical succession of ideas in rational thought or a fantastic parade in dream or imagination.

With this in mind, we can return to the mental state, the depth of which refers *inter alia* to its onset in instinctual drive. In primitive life forms or basic entities, the ground of becoming recurs for the organism or entity to replicate itself. Self-replication or causal persistence is essential for the individual to endure beyond one cycle of becoming. Causal persistence is an alternative to causal continuation as the basis of substance.[14] An object, a person, any entity, recurs each moment. How does a person, in spite of incessant change, remain more or less the same from one moment to the next? Causal persistence postulates a causal relation among spatiotemporal parts, while in process theory the persistence is due to the recurrence of a similar state. The theory of causal persistence merely reduces the replication of an organism to its temporal parts. In process theory, change is not a transition over states as spatiotemporal blocks, but lies in the becoming of a novel state. In causal persistence, one assumes that an object of some stability is a physical solid. When the object changes, we infer a change to

---

[14] Compared to the extensive literature on causal progression in Western and Asian philosophy, little attention has been given to causal persistence (see Russell, 1948).

the object and seek a cause for the change. An object that does not change does not need a cause for it to remain the same, but every object changes whether or not change is noticeable.

2. Note on Evolution

Microgenesis follows evolutionary process with particulars sculpted from possibility. Evolution is a population dynamic in which selection pressures trim excess or redundancy to fitness. This dynamic is internalized — or evolutionary theory is microgenesis externalized — in the recurrence of intra-psychic states, where excess is potential for variation and fitness is the parsing of excess to conform to adaptive pressures. Fitness as the goal of speciation is equivalent to definiteness as the goal of microgenesis. Extra-psychic elimination corresponds to intra-psychic parsing. Diversity in potential is non-existent possibility. Multiplicity in the onset and outcome of transition is an achievement of creative energy in formativeness. Creativity in the final object exemplifies novelty in actualization.

A sculpting model of mind such as microgenesis, or an evolutionary account of constraints on adaptation,[15] explains thought in terms of variation and selection, or abundance and elimination, the failure of unfit exemplars to survive and reproduce. This might suppose that experience, for better or worse, configures innate or early-acquired skills with a widespread potential for creativity that is linked to everyday cognition, with developmental and environmental conditions determining the degree to which potential is nourished or realized. The proliferation of forms that gives variation in populations, with parsing of maladaptive organisms, illustrates the creative potential in nature.

Evolution is a theory of speciation, not mental process, yet features of evolutionary dynamics appear as internalized attributes of the mind/brain state, such as the partition and sculpting of novel form from categories. Indeed, it may be that intrinsic features of becoming, such as whole-to-part or potential-to-actual transition, and self-replication (recurrence),

---

[15]   Constraints in evolutionary process are discussed by Deacon (2011).

provide an internal model for the population dynamic that is played out in the external world. Put directly, we speak of evolutionary process as the origin of species or, more widely, of organic life, but beyond a theory in Darwin's mind, what is the origin of evolutionary process? Specifically, why is there a process of evolution to begin with, and what accounts for its features? The possibility explored here is that the recurrence theory of change provides a template for thinking about self-replication as the basis of the population dynamic that characterizes evolutionary process.

We know that self-replication traces down to the most primitive organisms—viruses, prions—but it also occurs with crystal formation (Deacon, 2011). I would contend that such empirical evidence for self-replication, including autogenetic phenomena, is the outward sign of the recurrence that is the essential fabric of change. The cycle of recurrence of all things, with all objects and entities persisting by way of auto-iteration, is the foundational nature of change, a process that is universal but concealed within the outward flow from state to state. The interpretation of states as bounded and substance-like gives the impression of causal process in transition, and of causal necessity as the propulsive force behind forward advance. But inside the causal account lurks a deeper theory of change, in which the endpoints of recurrence are perceived or inferred as causes and effects, while actual change is in the realization of the state and its replacement, not across actualities deposited in the formative process.

The primacy of the struggle to reproduce, which for micro-genesis is recurrence extended to progeny, is reinforced by the importance ascribed to sexual drive. I have argued that hunger, for self-replication, is the primary drive, with sexuality, for progeny, secondary (Brown, 2012). The recurrence and becoming-into-being of all individualities, which is the universal basis of change, corresponds to the reproduction of progeny at the heart of evolutionary process. The hypothesis is that the externalization of intra-psychic process to interaction in populations is prior to the internalization of a population dynamic to intra-psychic process. With respect to the balance of deviation and replication in evolutionary stability and advance, the survival of individuals is an accessory to the replication of progeny. The individual can be sacrificed for the perpetuation of the species. What counts in evolution is the survival of a species, to which the individual is subordinate. Since the point of survival is to survive long enough, and competitively, to reproduce, self-replication will be secondary to reproduction. In contrast, all organisms show self-preservative behavior. For the individual organism, moment-to-moment recurrence is primary with the reproduction of others a secondary phenomenon or byproduct.

Consider for a moment the following: The theory of evolution as conceived by Darwin is a powerful model of population growth and change. However, the central features of evolutionary process can also be applied to the nature of human thought. An act of cognition begins in drive-potential and ends in a subjective or intra-psychic aim. Drive categories in the human mind have the capacity for an exuberance of form that is progressively trimmed to an adaptive endpoint by inner and outer constraints. The selection of acts and objects over a series of categories in the mind/brain state, as with evolution, can lead to anomaly (hallucination, irrationality), habitual outcomes or an advance into novelty. Aberrant thought, as in psychosis or retardation, is a kind of mutation that threatens survival. A veridical object individuates to fitness in the world, like an organism that adapts to the surround. Sensibility is to cognitive specification as the environment is to the survival of organisms, while recurrence of mind/brain states corresponds to reproductive success. Put differently, sensibility parses out irrelevant or maladaptive form — in thought, act and object — so that actualities in cognition map to the external world. The emerging construct is sculpted at successive phases to conform to external states of affairs. In evolution, the environment shapes behavior and eliminates organisms that are not successful adaptations. Environmental pressures on evolutionary adaptation correspond to the effect of sensibility on acts of cognition.

Features of microgenesis that were assumed to be outcomes of brain evolution or subjective analogues of extra-personal interactivity can as well be conceived as a model for evolutionary theory. Moreover, the application of the epochal theory of recurrence to inorganic events, e.g. replication of crystals, entails that a "self-replication" must be primary, with the evolution of DNA providing a means for group-selection and the continuance through others of the life of like-individuals. This leads to the idea that the individuation of mental contents in the mind/brain state externalizes in the selection of organisms that interact in the world. *In sum, the theory of microgenesis is projected, or intuited, as the basis of the discovery of evolutionary process, while the latter extends to popula-tions the recurrence theory of inorganic entities. Evolution is linear or serial, largely uni-directional (non-reversible) with branching. Micro-genesis is cyclical and recurrent with state-replacement, also uni-directional with branching. There is an obvious correspondence of speciation in evolutionary progression and specification in cognitive recurrence. Evolution is a theory of the origin of species, but micro-genesis might be the origin of the concept of evolution. That is, the continuum from lower organisms to human mind/brain raises the question of whether inherent features of inorganic nature extending into animate systems and fully realized in the human mind/brain are the origin of the concept of evolutionary process.*

3. Summary

To review to this point: the general problems and features of creativity have been discussed, as well as the concept of novelty as a universal of change. From this standpoint, creativity is an intermittent accentuation of inherent novelty, not only in human thought but in organic and physical nature. However, before considering creativity in terms of mind/brain process, or novelty in physical nature, it was important to examine causality as the dominant theory of change. On a variety of grounds, the theory of causation was found to be inadequate and incompatible with novelty in process or creativity in thought. Specifically, causal determinism does not make room for genuine novelty, much less a radical creativity, both of which are not only impediments to, but possible refutations of, causal progression. Causation assumes continuity over causal pairs leaving the actual transition or transfer from one state to another unexplained. Cause and effect are isolated as substance-like entities, while transition, inferred but unobservable, decants to properties of imaginary solids. A theory of recurrence is a more powerful account of continuity and identity, in that it can incorporate local causation, and also addresses the actual transition from before to after.

The discussion shifts to a process model (microgenesis) of the mind/brain state in which recurrence or self-replication,[16] whole-part analysis and sensory adaptation are the primary vehicles of (creative) transition in the evolution and development of life forms, minds and organisms. Unconscious segments in the mind/brain state and their precursors in lower organisms introduce the evolutionary concept of speciation by the parsing of redundancy, competitive interaction, elimination and selection of the fittest. Objects and organisms are selected by constraints on form so as to map to the immediate surround. The analogy of evolutionary process to the mind/brain state implies a potential application of evolutionary thought to theories of creativity, or the relevance of the concept of "creative evolution" (Bergson, 1911) to creative outcomes in human thought. The relation of evolutionary process to creativity has been discussed by others, and to an extent validated, but this can be explored more precisely in relation to microgenetic process.

Finally, the processual structure of the mind/brain state as an intra-psychic theory of individual change is shown to correspond with features of evolutionary process as an extra-psychic theory of population growth. This raises the intriguing possibility that evolutionary theory arose in the mind of its creator not only as a way of explaining diversity but also as an extension of patterns of intra-psychic process to extra-psychic events.[17] In this respect, similar to the role of explicit theory in

---

[16]   Understood as a recurrent state or epoch.

[17]   Other instances of interpretation that plumb the depths of mind to employ microgenetic concepts for seemingly unrelated topics include the origin of religious beliefs (Brown, 2015). An example is the interpretation of the trinity by Jakob Boehme, with god as potential, Christ as actual, and the holy ghost as the process of transition. Another example in the same category is the mystical Judaic belief in the creation of the world as going

scientific or other fields, microgenesis might serve as a covert or implicit guide to empirical discovery. Of course, one could as well maintain that microgenesis realizes evolutionary process as a culmination of its main features; i.e. as a basis of evolutionary change, an evolutionary outcome, or a conception of the human mind/brain as part of organic nature and an example of evolutionary process at work.

With this in mind, we can turn to the essential nature of recurrence and continuity, their relation to habit, novelty and transition, and the sources of creativity in human mentality, organic life and material nature.

4. Transition and Novelty

The actual transition from cause to effect, or from one epochal state to another, is unobservable. This difficulty is insurmountable in causal theory, in which cause and effect are marked off as discrete particulars, such that change is a bridge across two boundaries. The problem is finessed by postulating a change in properties that can, in principle, be specified. If the properties are unchanged, cause and effect are the same, but if different, this still leaves opaque the transition from one set of properties to another. In a word, the transition across properties is as ill-defined as that between objects.

To a great extent this difficulty is resolved in recurrence with overlap, since the overlap mitigates the problem of an empty interval, while the shaping or configuring effect of the antecedent on its successor explains transition as a conformance of effect to cause. This account does not involve properties, which are, at best, descriptors of endpoints of state-realization, nor the internal dynamic or becoming of state-formation, which is the actual locus of change. Put differently, in treating cause and effect as insular states, or objects with properties, causation ignores the genuine change and revision in the intrinsic process of actualization.

---

from not-nothing to an indefinite something, an idea also found in the Würzburg studies on the genesis of thought.

For both theories, the minimal state of an entity is modular, but for microgenesis the module is epochal, which means that the state or entity is not a product but a becoming with a diachronic history. Segments traversed in the recurrence of an entity undergo change at successive phases, each subject to revision, i.e. change (novelty) occurs at every phase in becoming. The transition restricts the degrees of freedom in recurrence, as in the refinement of potential or delimitation of possibilities, but it is not a causal force applied to the effect. It may be that constraints, *contra* Hume, are a species of cause, but unlike paradigmatic causation, the effect is what remains (persists) after an elimination of alternative paths. Since the ensuing state is embedded in the present one, i.e. the pre-decessor in its successor, the combination of overlap and recurrence across contiguous epochs is biased toward sameness or identity and is a restriction on difference or novelty. In sum, transition is not A to B but A becoming B through a fresh revival. The model for this, causal-persistence, is the prototype for all forms of causation, i.e. seriality is change in repetition. Bergson (1911) wrote, "…there is no essential difference between passing from one state to another and persisting in the same state."

Novelty is not mere difference. Every state is different from all preceding states, but difference only becomes novel when it is indeterminate and not a result of necessity. Complexity and contingency accentuate difference but genuine novelty, which is not due to covert resultants, entails a shift to quality and transition from a focus on quantity and measurement. Genuine novelty is an uncovering of what is concealed, not a re-shaping of constituents. The root source of the authentically new is unpredictability in partition. Sensibility gives difference, but change in becoming gives novelty. The one depends on external constraints, the other on the individuation of categories. The partition is not a selection of particulars encased within containers but the elicitation of virtual-parts from wholes as categories that are essentially inexhaustible.

In the becoming-into-being, categories enfold a multiplicity of *virtual*, formless or unrealized members, which refer to active or latent (potential) configurations of variable synaptic strength. Selection is driven by constraints within the category that reflect habit, exigency, the preceding state and the variable relations of meaning, shape and so on. Continuous change within the state and the novelty of the epoch are effected by absorption of the past into the present and the distillation of the external world in sensibility. These influences on becoming guarantee a similarity across contiguous states, but also ensure that no state will be an exact duplicate of another. For that to occur, a state of the brain or any entity would have to recur in every detail, as would the surrounding state of the world.

The distinction of novelty and difference is not trivial in that it depends on a theory of change. Difference, which is generally assumed to be causal, as in a re-bundling of constituent elements, implies a re-configuration of causal parts. In this respect, difference is the appearance of change, contrasted with sameness, which is always an approximation. As sameness is inexact resemblance, difference is superficial novelty. Novelty is contrasted with difference, which it subsumes, not sameness. The difference in states that passes for novelty is in the final actualities, not in novelty, which runs all the way through an epoch. That is, novelty appears at all phases in becoming, each phase representing a whole-part or category-item transform. Novelty, unlike causation, pertains to the final product — the subjective aim — which in the case of difference is the basis of comparison. Novelty is the dynamic of transition that carries an entity to existence, not as a conveyance but a becoming-into-being.

More precisely, excluding backward causation and isotropic time, i.e. if passage is irreversible, there is no possibility of sameness in either causation or recurrence, though the perception of sameness, which is essential to the stability of self and world, can be explained by the category-belongingness of every object or mental content. That is, if objects are concepts or categories, the resemblance of repeated object-experiences will reflect the elicitation of member-items that share common properties. Still, there is no exact recurrence. Difference is implicit for both causality and for process theory, in every existent and at every moment. The impossibility of exact recurrence gives difference by default. Even in a repetitive movement such as tapping the finger or a tremor, or a chair that one sees every day, each cycle of activity leaves traces in memory, however infinitesimal, that alter the organism, minimally (it is a fraction of a second older), not to mention other contents in the mind, and change in the passage of the world. In contrast, novelty is not a product of causal linkage or change in world-state but is intrinsic to becoming. The appearance of a changing world obscures genuine change, which is not so much concealed as invisible because of its uniformity.

A thing is not a bundle of fixed particulars but a microtemporal transformation at multiple segments as it actualizes. The nature of becoming is critical to the nature of change. More strongly, the basis of genuine novelty is the basis of apparent change in successive states. Intrinsic novelty is apprehended as the difference of one state from another. We perceive objectifications, not the change buried in them. Genuine novelty is not difference, which is as specious as sameness, though this is not to say it is not a problem for interpretation. Genuine novelty, which is the freshness of a state that is not a consequent of antecedents, is interior and qualitative.

Novelty is not possible in causal transmission since in principle even if the transition is opaque the effect is fully given in the cause. In contrast, change in the transition from potential to actual, as a focus within becoming, leads to genuine novelty in the arousal of unforeseen contents from what are essentially limitless categories, in which unlikely possibilities tend to be eclipsed by inner and outer constraints. The strength of constraints on categories establishes the degree of sameness or difference across states. A becoming that is highly constrained by past states, by habit and sensibility, will be roughly the same as its antecedent, while one in which constraints are loosened can show significant derailment. The effect of the prior state is essential in that it gives coherence to transition, but a withdrawal from the sensory world and an avoidance of habit are the instigators of creative thought. This makes it likely that the passivity so often recorded in creative thinking is not entirely in the object but partly in the laxity of constraint in its arousal.

In the becoming-into-being the final object or entity is preceded by the individuation of parts-as-sub-categories from wholes-as-superordinates, with each elicitation except the final one, and even that, serving as a sub-category for further partition. For example, when we look at a tree, the object, like the concept that precedes it, is a category of implicit parts. If we focus on a leaf or branch, the parts, e.g. veins, bark, are potential categories for still further partition. To delve into the figural prominence[18] of any part of any object—the inner and outer segments of an object-development—is to explore the categorical nature of part and whole in mind and world. Depending on constraints at each phase, there are multiple opportunities for deviation from expectation. The organism must achieve a viable balance between the rigid control of sensibility and the variation inherent in potential at successive points.

The individuation of categories, I would argue, is governed by a single law or algorithm that regulates a cascade of qualitative whole-part shifts or category-item transforms, in which the same operation occurs at successive segments. The hypothesis that a common algorithm governs partition at successive phases has greater explanatory power, parsimony and aesthetic appeal than the assumption that multiple operations are applied to different contents at different loci. This is also a distinction of internal and external relations. For example, the specification of preliminary acts and objects out of drive-categories, or of pre-objects out of object-concepts, or words out of lexical concepts, follows the same pattern as the selection of featural detail in objects, or the sequence of phonemes to "fill in" segments in abstract lexical frames. It seems likely that this process is not reinstated at different levels in microgenesis but comprises a traveling wave that is continuously iterated from onset to finality, from core potential to actual object. Since the phase-transition in the mind/brain state is a passage from before to after without a past or present, which appears on completion, there are no resting points between the before of one segment and the after of another, so that, even if the neural formations that mediate the transition appear discontinuous,

---

[18] The relation to the largely forgotten Gestalt theory should be evident (see Koenderink, 2015).

there should be no break in the continuity of successive partitions.

The regularity of whole-part shifts and, presumably, their universal application to both organisms and material entities, justifies the conclusion that the process is lawful, patterned and foundational in mind and nature. This does not mean that a law or rule directs transition in the manner of a putative grammatical rule. The lawfulness of the process does not translate into a law that is responsible for its regularity. Rather, lawfulness is extracted from regularity. In fact, the whole-part relation in human mind/brain appears to derive from developmental or morphogenetic process, e.g. parcellation, in which patterns of anatomical growth — sculpting of excess or redundancy — establish "force lines" that begin early in life with elimination, pass later on to inhibition, and continue as the individuation of categories by constraints in the mature organism.[19] Each stage entails specificity not by direct selection but by elimination or suppression of competing possibilities.

If the whole-part transition is lawful, universal and applicable to basic entities as well as organisms, wholes as categories are not intra-psychic inventions or explanatory tools, but operations of the human brain applicable to ancestral forms, that is, features of all living and inanimate things. Thus, in a hypothetical atom, the whole or category of the atom is the minimal duration or epoch that constitutes its being or existence. For an entity to exist is for the entity to become what it is over a duration of becoming. In basic entities, the whole or category is the epoch, while the parts are phases in the cycle of transition that reconstitutes the entity as a whole. In more complex systems, the whole-part shift is continuous over phases, with the entire transition comprising an irreducible state of an organism and its momentary existence. In an atom, this whole

---

[19]   Specificity in morphogenesis occurs by loss of cells and connections (e.g. Ebbeson, 1984). This continues in maturation to the inhibition of established contacts. The sculpting of an act of cognition represents the continuation of this trend in the actualization of the mind/brain state. Force lines laid down in fetal growth determine the pattern of later cognitive activity. See Brown (2015) for citations and documentation.

or category corresponds to a complete cycle or revolution, while the parts constitute the collective transition-points or segments that are traversed by an orbiting electron.

This observation, the birth of actuality in potential, is confirmed by the analysis of symptoms as shifts from potential to actual or whole to part that are not ordinarily accessible to introspection. Since a symptom is a fragment of mentality related to some portion of brain, it represents a microcosm of the mind-brain relation. Studies of pathology of the mind/brain reveal that symptoms can be understood as samplings of categories at different phases in an act of cognition. The symptom is not a guess, anomaly or aberration of merely anecdotal interest but is a clue to the relation of mind to brain. It also provides insight to the evolution and ontogenesis of the mind/brain and, in microgenesis, the basis of a theory of becoming that, by implication, extends mature cognition to patterns of fetal growth, as well as to more primitive forms. The more speculative aspect of this theory is that mental activity, fetal growth patterns and the relation to evolutionary process represent a continuation of the laws of change in organism to material process in nature. The relation of whole to part, the categorical nature of mind, and the fact that features of the human mind/brain evolve from animal cognition, justify an explanatory descent from human brain to more primitive species, even to physical nature. This way of thinking reverses the usual mode of reasoning that, in the promise of ultimacy, reduces all observation to physics, whether it begins or ends in psychology. In contrast, the argument here is that understanding the phenomenology of human mind in all its complexity and at the "highest" grade of activity uncovers patterns of process that apply to the most basic level. In a word, microgenetic theory is a paradigm for a new approach to physics.

Chapter 5

Microgenesis and Process Philosophy

Agency is feeling things becoming what they are.
Becoming is feeling as the possibility of what becomes.

While this chapter is not intended to be a commentary on the principal figure of process philosophy, Alfred North Whitehead, there are many points of contact between microgenetic theory and his process theory, all arrived at independently, especially concerning the concept of creativity and the related theory of concrescence. The two approaches — microgenesis and concrescence — converge on a similar idea from different, indeed opposing, perspectives. As I wrote in a prior article (Brown, 1998), *"Whitehead based his metaphysics on quantum features of the material world and gave us the grounding of a philosophical psychology. A beginning with psychology, however, can lead to insights on physical process not anticipated by science. There is a deep consolation in the fact that the laws of mind and nature are reciprocally discoverable, and that both manifest the activity of thought."* In the present work, novelty is assumed to arise in a universal process of becoming common to minds and physical entities, while creativity refers to the episodic accentuation of novelty in gifted individuals. Genuine novelty is a universal, while creativity is an occasion of its enhancement. However, for Whitehead, creativity is a foundational property of transition in mind and nature. Thus, a word about this distinction is warranted.

Microgenesis derives from clinical studies, primarily neuro-psychology,[20] but shares many features with Whitehead's idea of *concrescence* in spite of the clinical origin of one and the metaphysics of the other. The similarity merits discussion in relation to creativity as a universal. If creativity in this sense were equivalent to novelty as discussed, its universal nature would not be in dispute. However, in ordinary usage, creativity comes in many forms and degrees, and implies an original product, while novelty, in its uniformity and subtlety, refers to the inherent newness that arises in the formation of epochal states. In basic entities, repetition seems the rule and novelty is minimal. In more complex systems, the multiplication of parti-tions facilitates the scope and degree of novelty as a manifesta-tion of change. Novelty is intrinsic to becoming in all things, while creativity is commonly attributed to creative individuals. Moreover, unlike novelty, which is uniform and intrinsic, creativity implies a creator, whether the act of a creative indi-vidual or the creative power of god.

For Whitehead the category of creativity is final and all-encompassing — arguably a transcendental — and termed "sub-stantial activity." The ultimacy is processual, and has been compared to Aristotle's "matter", Spinoza's "substance" and Heidegger's "being." Concrescence captures the process-nature of being. Within process, whole/part relations form a category of creativity, a coming-together of the many into the one to form a novel occasion. Whitehead (1933) writes, "…this actual world… this real potentiality… as a whole is active with its inherent creativity, but in its details it provides the passive objects which derive their activity from the creativity of the whole. The creativity is the actualization of potentiality, and the process of actualization is an occasion of experiencing."

Though Whitehead speaks of the inherent creativity of the whole, he adds that creativity is the actualization of poten-tiality. The "creativity of the whole" could refer to the change in one epoch from its predecessor, or it could imply a source in potential from which "passive objects" arise. Creativity of the

---

[20] See Hanlon (1991).

whole is similar to the product-centered account of creativity and, except for the prehension of parts to wholes, adds little to the understanding of the creative process. The argument for creativity in actualization implies the selection of novel entities in a category.

1. Synthesis and Specification

In Whitehead, creativity is an inherent property of the coalescence of the many to the one. The many are taken to be objects, events, happenings, not only in an experiential state but also in the widest sense, i.e. as a convergence on an entity in a space-time continuum that creates a synthesis to ground the state that follows. The process of many–one fusion was estimated to occur about every 250 milliseconds, remarkably close to that of the perceptual moment hypothesis, or the minimal duration of a mental state. In process philosophy, creativity and many/one syntheses constitute universals that characterize all objects and entities. The relation of biology to physics is merely a matter of scale, since both exhibit the same part/whole relations and a progression to actuality over rhythmic or oscillatory phases, the energetics of which constitute feeling as the glue of passage.

For microgenetic theory, the opposite pattern is the case, namely the partition of the one to the many. The unity of the one is the relative consistency of the earliest segments of the state (or entity) guaranteed by the overlap of successive transitions (Fig. 2.1). One can speculate on the mind/brain state as a point in space-time, but a study of the state reveals, as William James wrote, that the ground out of which it develops consists largely of memory, not cosmic events, to which, one could add, sensory sculpting at several phases. It is not evident that the state arises in the synthesis of an immense multiplicity, which, in microgenesis, remains outside cognition. In a word, the state is fully endogenous with internal relations shaping the development, while the external relation to sensibility serves to delimit, not to fuse or integrate.

The elaboration of diversity from unity is the fundamental problem from the standpoint of mind, though an understanding of the synthesis of a many to a one, if it even occurs, would be equivalent to that of one/many specification. That is, how parts combine or emerge to form wholes is the same problem as how wholes divide or partition to ingredients. Whether organisms are conceived as part/whole syntheses or whole/part individuations, they are "structures" of rhythmic patterns, in which the energetics of oscillatory systems become the feelings that provide continuity within and across mind/brain states.

A refutation of the assembly theory of in-processing of sense data through which many/one synthesis is presumed to occur raises the question of the nature of the many and the precise means in the brain state by which fusion would occur. The synthesis of parts to wholes has been repeatedly postulated over the years but not, to my knowledge, cogently denied, with various hypotheses proposed as to how this might occur. Among the better-known ideas are prehensions, Lashley's (1951) concept of a scanner, and the hypothesis of a binding mechanism. These *ad hoc* speculations on an extraneous process or device, a rhythm or mechanism to accomplish the synthesis or integration of trillions of cells and connections, indicate the difficulty inherent in a synthesis that would bind together the multiplicity of brain events, not to mention those in a space-time manifold, through functions that are outside the data to be integrated.

In contrast, the microgenetic account of sensibility as a constraint on developing form helps to reformulate the many/one idea. The onset and ensuing development of an epoch of actualization represents a revival, not a synthesis, of the data of experience. The state is carved out of the data by the elimination of alternate possibilities. The overlap of contiguous states inclines initial phases in the epoch to iteration, with novelty in the course of a becoming-into-being induced by the influx of the immediately-prior state, by habit and by sensibility at multiple tiers in actualization. The central point is that sensory data are not ingredient in the assembly or synthesis of perception, which instead should be conceived as an endogenous image sculpted to actuality in conformance to a "niche" in the social and physical environment. Every perception-to-be runs a gauntlet of competing possibilities, with the analysis of categories decomposing residuals in each conceptual field as successive phases dissolve in the struggle of a forming object to adapt to the outer world. The immensity of events in a single perception—faces, landscapes, shadows, the evening sky—represent individuations within a single image, of a multiplicity of events in a momentary epoch, a striving to evolutionary fitness in which the environment (sensibility) parses out unfit forms to achieve an outcome that is most adaptive to external conditions. In the trajectory of an act of cognition, virtual or embryonic pre-objects fall aside at successive phases in the progressive elicitation of the final form.

Every existent, by virtue of being embedded in all local and cosmological events, is part of everything that exists at that moment, such that every event would seem to arise in relation to a vast surround of data. From this perspective, the idea of a many/one synthesis takes on a magnitude out of proportion to what actually occurs. The "butterfly effect" may be the case from a theoretical point of view, but a concrete occasion of experience takes place within a narrow window of circumstance. The epochal nature of the mind/brain state enfolds an intrinsic series that lays down a negative image of the real, but is largely insulated from the physical world, which surrounds the state like a garment, but does not go into its formation.

In metaphysical speculation, the creativity that inheres in many/one unification as an advance into novelty, and its universality of application, invoke the concept of deity as the ideal of togetherness and the ultimate creator of all things. The argument is that synthesis, as creative advance, is the measure of god's engagement with the individual and the universe. These speculations derive from the idea of a coherent totality or a oneness of all humanity, that applies an abstraction, in which concrete facts are charged with interconnectedness, to everything in the universe or, minimally, to the entire field of immediate experience. The concept of synthesis obligates a mechanism or process to explain unification, or to account for the coherence of isolates within the widest possible relatedness. However, the metaphysical commitment to a process or mechanism that implements synthesis, from an association of ideas to the impact on mind of events in inter-stellar space, has to contend with an interpretation of entities not as comings-together but as eliminations of irrelevancy.

A further difficulty with synthesis is the scope and generality of what comes together without a structure or rationale to delimit the outcome. In the absence of a rule or strategy to order or prioritize data in the whole, a synthesis of parts gives an open-ended assortment, not a unified whole, since the parts that can bind together are essentially limitless, regardless of the means of binding. Microgenesis takes a more conservative stance and is closer to evolutionary theory, in proposing relative constancy at the base of a mental state, with specificity achieved by individuation, not aggregation.

The pathology of cognition acts as a restraint on meta-physical speculation in exposing a qualitative change in the internal and unconscious segments of act and object formation. The symptoms of pathology can be sorted into a series that corresponds to a micro-temporal transition from wholes to parts, not the reverse. This is not to say that synthesis does not occur but that the specification of unities to multiplicities is the more fundamental event. This transition, described as a shift from category to member, can be further simplified to a focus on a specific and fairly typical occurrence that has been repeatedly documented (Brown, 1988), namely the arousal of a word, i.e. an abstract lexical frame, from a semantic category, and the specification of phonemes to fill in, and give flesh to, the word that arises. An understanding of the whole/part process by which an abstract lexical item is "selected" from a category, or phonemes "selected" to turn a word category into a concrete fact, would go a long way to explaining the opposite process of the synthesis of parts to wholes, if such a process occurs.

To take a concrete example, we can presume that a word such as *chair* is not *in situ* in the category *furniture*. The word, prior to its phonological realization, does not actually exist, other than as an abstract sub-category "given up" or trans-formed in the passage to a phonological representation. Indeed, no phase in the development of the word achieves actuality until the transition is complete. Antecedent phases have virtual existence in mind or in the world as precursors in the epochal state(s) in which the word *chair* actualizes. This includes core activation and successive zeroing-in within nested categories, to that of *furniture,* which, though implicit in the elicited member, e.g. *chair,* is itself unrealized except in transit to the final item. In other words, every phase in speaking or thinking the word *chair* resolves out of an object-concept and semantic categories, which are wholes to the individuation of further parts, as the entire sequence is winnowed down to final definiteness.

The specification of a word from a category is not like picking candies from a jar, i.e. filling empty slots in a word-frame. Prior to phoneme selection, the word is indefinite, probabilistic, qualitative, unbounded, acausal and indeterminate. The potential for errors in word choice or phoneme-realization reveal the possibility, thus the novelty, in the selection process. In effect, possibilities emerge prior to finalities with other possibilities unborn. Whether a target such as *chair* issues from the category, or another word in the same category such as table, or a word in the sub-category of the target, such as throne or palanquin, depends on the fine structure and attributes of the category. Unexpected words can be errors or creative departures, and can occur at the level of the phoneme, the word, the phrase or the idea. In each case there is specification of sub-ordinate possibilities from a more inclusive whole.

It is clear that the whole/part shift in psychological study is based on brain activity, such that specification of parts from wholes refers to a physiological process in brain, perhaps similar to lateral-inhibition, or the center-surround and field effects in the Gestalt concept of the figure/ground relation. The possibility of an isomorphism of brain process with cognitive phenomena has been discussed previously. The concept of a rhythmic or vibratory activity that runs from mind to nature, from brain to superstrings, implies that oscillatory systems in brain also undergo whole/part fractionation, for example, a series of harmonics in relation to action, music and language. The transformation of isotropic energy to anisotropic feeling, the oscillatory nature of energy and the rhythmic layering of the mind/brain, i.e. the sequence of kinetic rhythms parsed to successively finer melodies, points to the role of feeling in the manifestation of process and the affective tonality of concepts, such that feeling, as the derivative of energy, is the process of becoming through which the partition of categories leads to objects of value in the world. The conjoint development from the categorical primitives of drive and instinctual feeling to external objects of worth, from the inner core of the mind/brain state to its external surface, constitutes an epoch of becoming-to-being.

2. On Active and Passive

Whitehead writes that the objects that arise from potential are passive though the passivity is not, perhaps, in their arising, but this overlooks pre-objects at sub-surface phases. For microgenesis, passivity applies to objects when they detach to form an external world, but formative phases in the object, e.g. images, may be active or passive depending on a variety of factors. If objects that issue from potential are viewed as passive, the entire power in creativity rests in potential, or in the actualization of the object out of potential, not in what actualizes. This would be consistent with microgenesis and opposed to a product-centered account of creativity, but it is not altogether clear if this was Whitehead's point of view, nor that there was a detailed consideration of transition over the actualization process. If objects actualize directly from potential and are passive with no intermediate steps, at what point does creativity occur? Iteration over phases in selection, i.e. a wave of category-item transforms within each epoch, implies that the whole/part specification of potential constitutes the becoming-process, with forming objects serving as potential for ensuing transitions, each whole-part shift having the capacity for novel transformation.

Given that objects are usually conceived as impacting the organism through external sensibility, with the organism a passive recipient of environmental stimuli, irrespective of the fact that the organism "chooses" to perceive some sector of external space, clinical observations tend to be dismissed in theory-construction, at any rate, they are not accorded the significance they deserve. However, should it be conceded that objects are not initial data for objects assembled from "sensory input" but undergo passage in the mind to a phase when sensibility provides the final modeling, so that images take on meaning as markers of segments in a mind-world transition.

Objects also take on activity through a re-actualization of the potential in which they originate. We think objects are passive in relation to the self, consistent with their putative mind-independence, while actions are viewed as active or willed, even if their passivity is buried in the formative process. Covert agency in perception is uncovered when pre-objects do not objectify but remain as mental images, either passive or under voluntary control. In action, the feeling of agency, which is largely perceptual,[21] is emphatic at penultimate phases that deposit in the body. Unlike objects that detach as they externalize, actions objectify within the body, such that the volitional feeling derived from pre-act imagery now occupies the action (body image), which does not detach like an object, but is partly in the mind with a feeling of belongingness, while in perception the feeling that went into willing is now the value that passes into and belongs to the object.

Agency is voluntary action of the body, not action of the body on objects. In this sense, the body is comparable to an image that may or may not be accompanied by volitional feeling. Most actions, like objects, occur automatically, but the object appears fully in the world, except for pathological cases such as derealization, when the object has a dream-like quality. In contrast, action is partly in the world, partly in the mind, again except for pathology, as when a psychotic believes his actions are under external control. In perception, agency for images is lost at the mind-world boundary, though it is carried into and felt to empower certain objects that are no longer products of thought. The extension of agency to objects is seen in the attribution to other minds: human, animal, robot, as in pathology when agency is withdrawn, such as depersonalization.

---

[21]   The debate between Wundt and James on the *Innervatsionsgefühl* centered on the origin of the feeling of activity, which we now know comes from recurrent collaterals of the action discharge.

One can ask, what is the meaning of active? Is activity in the object, in its formation, in the potential from which it arises, or in the agency of the individual? The object may be active in the world but passive in the mind, i.e. not felt as volitional. Is "active" equivalent to purposeful? Is it intrinsic to the object? Is volition exercised on the object or is it ingredient? Is this dismissive of Bergson's claim that object-formation is an active, efferent process, which contradicts the conventional view that objects are passively received in the mind? Finally, are objects reconstructed from sensibility or does sensibility sculpt pre-objects in conformance with adaptive need?

For primitive organisms, active and passive are not clearly identifiable. Is a bird that eats a grub or a bee that searches for pollen showing active behavior, or, in spite of activity, exhibiting a passive response to sensibility combined with instinctual drive? Very primitive organic and inorganic entities are active or passive in a single transition over a complete epoch. In sessile organisms or plants, the forward direction of growth gives momentum and direction to what appears to be a passive entity. An elementary entity with limited opportunities for novel derailment can be assumed to be active or passive throughout its becoming: active with respect to self-replication or causal persistence; passive with respect to bonding or recombination. A new entity is also created when it "comes-together" with others. For example, liquidity is not a property of one molecule of water but of many, each inheriting novelty from the changing whole.

Within the mind/brain, formative phases, i.e. pre-objects, images, though intermediate in the completion of a full cycle, are no less active than actions. All imagery is perceptual, whether verbal (inner speech) or preparatory for action. The feeling of agency for visual images is no different from that for motility. The essential difference is that to be active in the world is to effect change on others, while to be active in mind is to have no effectuation on objects. Patients who lose motility can imagine movement but the loss of all sensation leads to paralysis. While some images are passive to the observer, i.e. non-agentive, they may be active in other ways, for example, as mobile dream images or as potential for further partitions. The image itself does not transform to an object; rather, the object individuates out of the potential to form an image, the image only appearing as an attenuation of that segment of mind/brain that gives rise to an object. The substrate of the image becomes potential for the object, which retains features of the segment that would have actualized had it been the final phase.

Some waking images are felt to lack volitional control, especially creative imagery, but others such as imagination images can be volitionally aroused and "manipulated." We can imagine a mouse crawling on the back of an elephant. Memory images can be active or passive. We can try to remember an experience, a fact, a feeling, not always with success, but once conscious of a memory, in contrast to forgetting, there is a feeling of some control. The point is, in its journey from mind to world, active and passive vary with different images at successive planes, e.g. memory, thought, eidetic, and within the image according to context. In other cases, such as dream and hallucination, an active response—gazing at an hallucination, holding on to a dream on waking—may result in the disappearance of the image.

Though Whitehead was thinking metaphysics, not psychology, a developing object achieves passivity in detachment when fully externalized, at which point agency or active power may transfer to the object. Psychosis offers many examples of this phenomenon. For example, in command hallucinations, the image is felt to speak to and control the individual. Conversely, a developing action is felt as less active prior to externalization, perhaps because discharge in the body is discharge in the image. With an arrest of action-development, the image as precursor is usually accompanied by indecision. That is, indecision, choice or uncertainty is a manifestation of imagery at a formative phase in action. A phantom limb moved in the imagination is similar to a real one. *The conclusion is that a feeling of activity or passivity is partly in the image, partly in the self (agency, receptiveness), and partly in the context and degree of realization (dream, after-image).* Finally, regardless of active, passive, phase or type, the individual is ordinarily not aware that an image or object arises from a category (potential) constrained to produce it, an observation that documents the fortuitous insight of process-philosophical speculation.

More generally, in spite of the active or passive quality of images, the elicitation of any content from a category is by suppression of alternatives, such that the individual does not select content but is a receptacle for what is evoked. The feeling of active search and selection is a result of conditions that constrain and, by default, give rise to content. Further, if active and passive inhere largely in the content, not the agent, in spite of the feeling of decisiveness the individual is a recipient for content accompanied by active feeling. This is of particular relevance to creativity, in which the individual is conscious of being passive to the arousal of original ideas. One can say that the lack of control in object selection, together with the quality of items selected, accentuate a feeling of passivity that is the hallmark of creative ideation.

3. Potential

Whitehead was not altogether clear on whether creativity resides in potential, or in the act of arising, or what arises, or what finally actualizes, or in the whole-part shifts that underlie concrescence. The ambiguity of potential, its lack of differentiation as a correlate of creative activity, turns objects into inert products and makes vagueness an explanatory strategy. The idea that creativity is in the actualization of potential is consistent with microgenetic theory, if potential is equivalent to category and parts to virtual members. Categories as phases in microgenesis conform to whole-part transitions in concrescence. Possibility in potential is not necessarily creative, only its evocation. Potential goes hand in hand with possibility, in that there is no given, and the virtual nature of contents is not explicable on a causal basis. The transition from possibility to actuality exhibits novelty regardless of whether the items evoked are creative. While possibility implies the arising of the unpredictable, it is not decisive as to whether the output is creative though it conforms to whole/part shifts as the vehicle of novelty.

Even with a conventional outcome, creativity relates to the category from which the content develops. A depiction of the contents of potential prior to their selection, were it possible, i.e. exhausting all possible contents of a category, would entail that potential is a mereological sum, or that categories and members are finite. To have knowledge of the contents of potential in advance of their selection, i.e. knowing the constituents or to-be-selected items, or an inventory of possible items waiting for partition, eliminates becoming and drains categories of creative force.[22] Conversely, the lack of specificity in a potential that is mere possibility without content is a kind of vacancy pregnant with possibility. Novelty would then arise from a kind of absence, a difficulty mitigated if potential is a category, since the constraints that delimit structure and induce partition give a semblance of form to what is otherwise empty and without direction.

In Whitehead, potential is a coming-together (prehension) and unification of the incipient many. He writes, "it lies in the nature of things that the many enter into complex unity", yet he admits that "the sole appeal is to intuition" (in Garland, 1983). How this occurs and what constitutes the many is unclear. There is also, as discussed, an ambiguity in whether creativity consists in virtual data that comprise potential or the selection of novel contents. The argument appears to be that multiplicity is resolved in the course of becoming to form the actuality of the one, with every unity a diversity of constituents prehended by feeling to achieve unification in the common realization of a present moment of existence. Feeling unifies multiplicity by binding together diverse data of experience. The final diversity, Whitehead wrote, is a novel one that is created in the actualization.

4. Concrescence and Microgenesis

Each entity has a quota of feeling that distributes into its parts, with myriad entities, e.g. cells, subcellular elements, melded together as "societies" to form new occasions. Entities and the

---

[22] This is, in fact, the position of the copy theory of memory and thought, as well as Freud's view on the recombination or becoming-conscious of modular traces.

systems in which they are embedded are novel states of existence, each occasion bringing constituents together in a becoming that partitions on completion to diversity. The diversity of outcome differs from the diversity at onset, though it is unclear which diversity is combined in the next occasion. For Whitehead, it would appear to be the final diversity that relinquishes objectivity in passage to an eternal object, while in microgenesis the next epoch, reinstated in the initial diversity, follows the track of the prior state.

Apart from experience of the object-field and the relevant material data, namely the innumerable physical occurrences that go into the existence of an organism or entity, what if any other substrate serves as a foundation for the next occasion? Diversity unified by feeling is apprehended in the coherence of the field, as are presumably the physical data that make up the observer, but how does the multitude of elements "come together" when each element has its own cycle of becoming? The coming-together is a problem that is not adequately resolved by a term such as "prehension", which refers to a mode of feeling. It seems likely that feeling is engaged in the fusion of multiplicity and the elicitation of particulars, but a deeper account of feeling in the course of actualization is required. Moreover, the creation of a "society" or an occasion of experience would seem to go beyond the activity of a given brain, organism or other entity to include the mind-independent world that impacts the organism and the sensibility that constrains the mind/brain state.

This is also the case in microgenetic theory, when the replacing occasion, which traverses essentially the same path as its antecedent, "comes together" by way of feeling to actualize a novel epoch. However, the microgenetic idea presumes individuation, not combination. Do entities come-together or arise out of a common ground? Combination by external relations seems obvious, but the alternative is access to an underlying field from which figural elements and internal relations are generated. Physical energy becomes feeling in organism as the force that unifies diversity at the onset of the state. Since all things devolve to and arise from feeling, coming-together can be interpreted as accessing the feeling common to all individualities.

Feeling guarantees and enlivens existence by distributing throughout entities and accompanying them into the perceptual surround. In every part-object, feeling is absorbed in successively larger systems or organizations, e.g. mitochondria, cell, tissue, organ, person, world, uniting a multitude of particulars into a construct from which a new state and its constituents arise. Of interest, the concept of a coming-together by feeling recalls the concept of time in Newtonian physics, where an infinitude of individual times, from a chronon to a brain state, are represented in absolute time. The inclusion of the temporal properties of particulars in the framework of an absolute time corresponds to the plenitude that is prehended in the duration of a momentary state. In concrescence, the world coalesces in an individuality, while in Newtonian time, individualities are absorbed in a universal. What is not clear in Whitehead is how a society of occasions becomes the sole occasion of an organism, or how a multiplicity of constituents is unified in the cycle of an individual epoch.

5. Perishing

For Whitehead, an actual object perishes into the past as an eternal or non-temporal object to serve as the ground of the next occasion.[23] The simultaneity of potential is equivalent to the non-temporality of the eternal. The past perceptual world, not its intra-psychic correlates or antecedents, is the datum from which the next world is fashioned. In microgenesis, the perceptual surface perishes, though certain of its precursors in memory are revived. States develop out of the residue of their predecessors. Due to the similarity of states at the onset and the coherence of sensibility at the outcome, there is compatibility across adjacent states. The revival of memory in human cognition provides constraints on replication. In human mind, memories are constitutive (structural) and representational

---

[23] For Whitehead, eternal means nothing more than non-temporal (Cobb, 2008).

(images). In physical entities, recurrence by memory is constitutive. The entity "remembers" itself into existence, each state being a remembrance of its antecedent.

At all phases in becoming, change is the seed of novelty; intrinsic, induced and dependent on the imaginal residue of a fading sensibility. The core of one actuality is the kernel of the next, not only for the final object but for all segments. Perishing opens the door to novelty, in that objects vanish to permit change in the oncoming epoch. Indeed, it is not well-appreciated that the perishing of epochs extends to the perishing of phases within the epoch, as each phase is absorbed in the next; that of word-meaning transitions to words, and words to speech sounds. An object-concept perishes in transitioning to objects. Phases that perish, unlike actualities, are essentially inexhaustible. Concepts are not diminished by giving objects. The concept does not achieve actuality yet is imminent in the final outcome.

The difference between the perishing of an object and the perishing of a phase within the object is that, in human mind, on completion of an epoch, the object has a past to perish into, whereas prior to completion there is paradoxical non-temporal succession—before and after—that actualizes all at once, becoming temporal as it perishes. Specifically, phases in the mind/brain state are earlier and later, though becoming is simultaneous until it terminates. Preliminary phases are traversed, but without a past they remain ingredient in the epoch. Since the final or actual object is not an isolate but comprises all phases in its development, the overlap of states preserves proximal segments so that the perishing affects primarily the distal portion (Fig. 2.1). Past and present are created as the present actualizes, allowing the actual object to slip into the past.

In sum, prior to termination phases are earlier and later but nontemporal, the earlier perishing in the later but not perishing absolutely, because the past of the phase does not yet exist. Early phases in the state never achieve existence, since they are replaced by the ensuing state prior to actuality. That is, at T-1, later (world-close) phases realize earlier segments, but the earlier are now those of T-2, or T-1 combined with T-2, since T-2 realizes early segments in T-1

*before T-1 actualizes. The early segments in a state transmit potential
to later segments, and in that sense are imminent when the state
actualizes, but an early pristine T -1 can never actually exist because
it is overtaken by T-2 prior to T-1 completion. The distal portion is
lost when the state perishes, while the proximal segments are constrained – replaced, sustained – by the state that follows. The distal
perishing is absolute, though intermediate phases can be recovered in
fresh revivals.*

What, then, can we say about the final object that perishes
but does not, except in theory as an eternal or Platonic object,
give rise to a consequent? The fate of the actual is to detach but
not as a mind-independent part of nature or novel sensibility.
Segments in the present facilitate recurrence, depending on
similarity of adaptation. Decay (incomplete revival) in memory
is not explained by conveyance to different stores or transformation of the original, but by the recapture of traversed
segments. The sequence in forgetting, to iconic, short-term,
then long-term memory, uncovers phases in the order of the
original perception. To remember an event is for the revived
image to actualize as a dominant segment within the complete
epoch. Ordinarily, the phase of imagery is transformed to an
object, but without recurrent sensibility, the state is revived to a
pre-terminal phase. Were this the final phase, not an accentuation embedded in a perception, the outcome would be dream.
Except for representation as an image, the major portion of the
revival is non-conscious, for only the superficial reaches a conscious plane.[24] The final object, the perceptual world, disappears in the past, not to be repeated except in a vivid eidetic
or similar sensibility, but early and intermediate segments do
recur in one form or another as the better part of the oncoming
state.

Take the example of attending to an object, say a tree in the
garden, which recurs by repeated adaptation to a relatively
fixed and coercive sensibility. The revived infra-structure, constrained by sensibility, gives a recurrent model of the tree. If
attention is diverted to another object, say a pond, earlier

---

[24]   The distinction of implicit and explicit, or procedural and declarative, is
relevant here.

segments in the perception of the tree are still revived but the final modeling is for the pond. The mixture of early phases in the present (tree) with incipient phases in the ensuing (pond), i.e. the tree as memory and the pond as perception, the early modulated by its successor, the later perishing when the successor (pond) actualizes, gives continuity to self and world.

Each state is sculpted by a different sensibility to a different outcome. If attention is attenuated or directed inward, say with the eyes closed and without external sculpting, the tree recurs as a memory image. Earlier phases in the antecedent state recur as images in the occurrent one. The tree in reflection or remembrance does not have the pictorial quality of its former endpoint, but recaptures the potential lost in the passage to an object. In this way, as an image of a past object, tree and pond, though not in immediate perception, continue by incomplete revival to influence the sources of memory, reverie and creative thought.

Sensory data force all phases of the epoch to continuously adapt to the outer world, the physical and the social. Genuine novelty, prior to adaptation, is attributable to the parsing of categories to unintended outcomes. In the course of actualization, novelty owes to the instantiation of the preliminary, i.e. sub-categories over the phase-transition. Transitional contents do not actualize but serve as potential for further partition. Potential is the unspecified depth of category. In the mind/brain state, core potential, e.g. the category of a drive, individuates to a sub-category, e.g. desire. Phases in the state, no matter the degree of specification, e.g. a word, are still potentials that pass in succession, a wave of whole/part transitions, with each sub-category individuating over phases in becoming. In the transition, there is no actual content until the state actualizes, or when the content becomes temporal until an epoch is realized at the endpoint—the final whole/part transition—of the series.

Since each individuation is qualitative, arising out of a shifting context (potential), subtle biases can give unexpected deviations at successive segments. Transitional "contents" do not have the reality of final actualizations, nor do they exist other than as implicit constraints, since antecedent phases do not deposit content, but are given up in the formation of the ensuing segment. As in dream, in which prior events or phases that vanish are recalled on waking, only the final actuality exists, though aspects of antecedents can be recovered on completion of the epoch. Since a phase in transition does not exist prior to the epoch, it is unreal, though the phase is implicit, and takes on realness in succession, when the actualization terminates. Since the final actuality, e.g. a word, is a category in which further partition is abated, the actuality, though existing for a fraction of a second, and consisting of an implicit series of formative phases, has greater realness as an existent in perspectival time, even if the agent is largely oblivious to these unconscious happenings. When the terminus of a transition is an external object, its apparent solidity, extra-psychic locus and mind-independence, reinforce the impression that final particulars are real—for some philosophers, the only real things—in a way that intra-psychic precursors are not.

In sum, early phases do not exist; the actual object, whether a dream or perception, is the final phase of an intra-psychic trajectory. The final actuality exists briefly, as an epoch that includes its microtemporal history, a history merged with the ensuing state. When later phases in T-1 perish, early phases of T-1 and T-2 also perish but those of T-2, as yet unrealized, do not perish absolutely but pass into subsequent phases. The object as an existent is no less real, no less illusory, than the entire sequence through which it develops. The fact that the major extent of the becoming entails a wave of potential without definite content distinguishes the particulars at the endpoint from the antecedent potentials. This accentuates the reality of final partitions at the expense of formative process.

Microgenesis, like concrescence, is a transition from potential to actual—a repeated partition of categories—but in contrast to concrescence, passage is from unity at the base to diversity at the surface. Initial unity owes to the relative homogeneity and focus of the categorical primes, while the unity in the final diversity owes to the coherence and common diachronic ancestry of surface finalities. The bedrock of the state may rest in the animal inheritance, or still earlier in the brain state, or in the physical processes of nature that embrace all individualities. If so, all organic life springs from the depth of a source category that might as well be the mind of god. Conceivably, community, society and the physical world are the effective ground from which the generality of drive and the uniqueness of organism surface. For Schopenhauer, individuals are ideas in the mind of god. If each instance of individuality arises from a universal ground, god or nature, a profound connectedness of all life on earth would be the basis of a shared humanity.

6. Creativity as a Philosophical Problem

Apart from process thinkers, creativity has not been a focus of philosophical study since the ancients invoked divine inspiration, effectively removing the topic from rational analysis. The emphasis on unconscious thought, on imagination and fancy, and on sudden insight, especially in the arts — keeping in mind Archimedes' cry of *Eureka* on solving the problem of volume estimation — defies the philosophical method of argumentation, which is meant to convince, not create, and the insistence on deductive reasoning and logic, which does not ordinarily lead to conclusions not subsumed in the premise. Reason examines and decides the truth of statements but does not bring forth new material. Indeed, a new idea in philosophy is almost a *non-sequitur* since it is science and psychology that invigorate novel problems and perspectives.

Additionally, the assumption that a philosophical problem has a rational explanation, or that rational judgment leads to creative outcomes, or that reasoning plays a part in creative discovery — not *post hoc* once discovery occurs — has limited application to the creative process. Even in science, where problem-solving differs from an original artwork, philosophy is at a loss to explain, for example, how the vision of a circle of snakes can lead to a theory of the benzene ring, or Loewi's dream that led to the demonstration of acetylcholine as a cardiac transmitter, or Einstein's fly on a train in relativity, that is, how ideas emerge and problems are solved in unconscious thought, or the role of imagination, metaphor and dream, when consciousness and rational thought are not engaged. Creativity challenges philosophy to take a larger view of thinking, to not just focus on mental statements or truth judgments and the like, but to adapt an approach that recognizes the depths and diversity of conceptual thought.

Apart from these philosophical problems, the nature of creativity and creativity in nature are fundamental to causation and theory of change. If universal novelty is genuine, and is sampled and expanded in human creativity, the underlying process of thought cannot be described as rational. Is reason a mode of argument that conforms to certain rules, or is it a natural mode of thinking, the patterns of which establish the rules? Is a reasoned argument restricted to consciousness or, more likely, does its content arise in the unconscious? It is also a matter of interest whether creativity in thought is allied to creativity in brain, or is emergent or epiphenomenal. Creativity raises questions as to how ideas arise, if not as some think by a mere rearrangement of parts. Does anyone actually believe that, by pure chance, an army of monkeys would eventually type *Hamlet*?

Though not precisely linked to creativity, there is also the question, in perception and thinking, of cross-modality. Brahms asked why he should go to the opera when he could stay at home in an easy chair and listen to the music reading the score. It is said that the well-known phonetician, Morris Halle, could hear speech from sound spectrograms. Is this just an ability of a highly-trained professional? Music is a language. Does hearing a score differ from hearing a poem in one's head when it is silently read? The same "translation" from the visual to the auditory is involved. Is this a complex form of synesthesia? Some years ago, I argued — cited in Cytovic (1989) — that the separate modalities of perception do not come together by association but individuate out of an archaic multi-modal source. How does this relate to theory of perception or thought?

Firstly, if this is the case, it supports the general principle of parcellation, with particulars related diachronically, not by interaction. *The reciprocal connectivity across phases in the actualization of the modalities is not for association but, in my view, serves to keep the momentary development of the senses in synch,* thus in the same mind and brain (Brown, 1988). Secondly, since every mental state arises over the diachronic sequence with

overlap and replacement, the shared data over early, intermediate and final phases in language and perception accounts
for the coherence of images and events. The fluid shift from
visual to verbal imagery, or the evocation of the visual imagination by inner speech and the reverse, are not finessed as a result
of mere association, but owe to the common origin and linked
derivation of all perceptual and action systems. In an art form
such as writing, verbal imagery plays a major role, in another
such as painting, visual imagery, but the writer will visualize a
scene to be depicted in poetry or prose and the painter will
engage in verbal musings on the progress of the work.

Finally, the source-unity and coherence of the modalities
gives a cross-modal confirmation of external reality, as well as
the internal world of dream. Any world seems real with a
consensus of the senses. Awake or asleep, to see, hear, feel and
smell or taste an object or object-field reinforces the limited
impact of, and inability to know, a real or imagined world
through a single perceptual system. In dream there is no
alternate world for comparison. Waking, we conclude that
dream is illusory. Is waking reality also an illusion compared to
a still further level of consciousness, e.g. a noosphere, or a
noumenal world beyond perception? More than dream,
waking brings the consensual feeling of realness into focus.
When we see a tree shaking in the wind, hear the rustle of the
leaves, feel the breeze on our face and taste the sweetness of the
air, we wonder if these perceptions are unified from the
beginning or are secondarily integrated as a whole by blind
association. In my view, only unity at the onset of the mental
state explains the coherence. Finally, these comments raise a
wider point that I have previously addressed, namely the
analysis into parts and corruption of temporal relations in the
pipedream that the whole can be reconstructed from its
elements. Experiments done long ago by Sperry, Pribram and
others put to rest the mistaken concept that cortico-cortical
associations are essential to behavior, yet the idea survives in
modularity and componential theory. Philosophy has a role to
play in exposing the fraudulent bases of these claims.

Chapter 6

Novelty

The more real a thing, the more illusory,
The more illusory, the more real it may be.

Ordinary science entails an ontology of being that manages reasonably well without novelty or creativity, since it supposes atomic entities that do not undergo intrinsic change. The process approach is critical to an understanding of mind in relation to nature, in that it incorporates the part/whole relation—in brain activity, psyche and inanimate nature—as a fundamental pattern in the formativeness (becoming) through which individualities are created. The basis of change from moment to moment is in the fractionation of entities and the embodiment of becoming in an epochal state. The epoch is an indivisible or atomic "structure" of transient existence on completion.

Novelty in change is a constant that is concealed in the uniformity and universality of continuous transformation, in mind and in passage in the world. Creativity heightens novelty and raises it from something implicit (a tacit, invisible norm of passage) to something explicit (works of exceptional insight and beauty). The contiguity inferred by Hume to depend on mind for causal power is consistent with a theory of replacement. The assumption of causation in mind-external, i.e. in external objects, is an interpretation, from the standpoint of external objects, of the becoming from potential to actual in mind that gives rise to the objects. The genuine change of becoming is not available to conscious perception, but is apprehended as causal in consciousness.

Genius is conceived as inexplicable precisely because becoming is opaque to conscious mind. There is also inattention to novelty in change as the mode of qualitative advance. A characteristic of universal novelty and its offspring, creativity, is that the creative is not reducible to, nor can it be deduced from, what is already known (Rapp, 1990). Genuine novelty does not reshuffle the cards of prior occasions. There is also a blindness to transition and a powerful tendency to focus on stabilities, not *relata* or gradients, such that process, transition or becoming are conceived as extrinsic to mental solids. This inattention to process is exemplified in the problem of causal transmission, with creativity displaced to the product away from the process through which it develops.

1. A Note on Emergence

If causation is not a legitimate model for novelty in change or creative thought, can we consider novelty as an emergent of causal process, even if probabilistic, not only in the evolutionary progression to human brain or process within the brain, but also in the elaboration of psyche from brain activity? Emergence could also explain the novelty in creative thought but not on a probabilistic basis. Emergence could refer to some aspects of mind, such as language or imagery, rather than mind as a whole, but one still has to account for the coherence of emergent phenomena. There are several ways of thinking about emergence in relation to causation and novelty and these require some discussion before the problems of novelty and creativity are considered.

Emergence as a product of covert resultants is consistent with causal theory. The emergence of "higher" levels, as in systems theory, would occur through compounding of (hypothetical) causal pairs—basically, reflexes—that are concealed within the complexity of the transition. Even in simple oscillatory systems (Dewan, 1976), the emergence of a novel oscillator is presumed to be causal in spite of uncertainty over the actual transition, though if it is not causal the emergent step still remains obscure. In the evolution of novel forms, genetic and epigenetic factors interact with environmental sculpting to create a complex set of conditions, largely unanalyzable, in which an outcome appears emergent because the multiplicity of incremental steps is of such magnitude and diversity as to defy elucidation. The postulate that causal resultants underlie emergence merely inserts hypothetical "place-holders" to explain an occult transition. This does not account for emergence, but only denotes a phenomenon, i.e. causation, no less in need of clarification than that which it purports to explain. For the sake of scientific intelligibility, causally-based emergence decomposes the inexplicable to the unverifiable through an implicit sequence of invisible steps.

Another example of emergence explained on the same basis is that from brain to mind. Here it is less a question of lower to higher than of how a physical substratum can generate psychic experience. While it may be the case that when we examine specific features of mind, such as speech, reading and so on, we can identify intermediate stages, emergence is invoked as an explanatory concept even if there is no accounting for the appearance of mind or subjective experience from physical process. The possibility of an isomorphism of whole-part shifts in mind and brain is explored in Brown (2014).

With respect to creativity, or thought generally, the selection of an item (sub-category) must navigate layered fields of meaning-relations with multiple routes of development and potential derailment by way of overlapping attributes and analogies within and across categories, especially in accounts lacking a subjective aim to achieve a desirable target. The infrastructure of word, object or act specification and the transit through this complexity, or the actualization of the mind/brain state over phases, can be inferred from errors occurring in patients with brain damage, which sample the process at a depth beneath the threshold of consciousness.

The specification of phonemes to fill in the virtual slots in abstract lexical frames is a qualitative individuation of wholes into constituents corresponding to the shift from whole (category, frame, context, ground, etc.) to nested (but not constitutive) parts (items, members, particulars, content, etc.). This shift can be construed as emergent in the partition of unity to multiplicity, or generality to definiteness. The reverse process, a transition from part to whole, would exhibit the same properties, and serve as a model for emergence. As Heraclitus said, "the road up and the road down are the same road."

However, the shifts need not be "vertical" from higher to lower or the reverse, but "horizontal", as in the purported emergence of mind from brain.

If one were to define the whole-part shift in qualitative terms, not as a mapping across "solids" or a series of embedded but concealed resultants, one would have the outline of a theory of emergence. More precisely, an account of the whole/part shift in qualitative and non-fractal terms is also an account of the reverse transition from part to whole. In my estimation, such an account in psychological or mathematical form would give the foundational operation of the mind/brain. The whole-part shift, conceived as an iterated cascade from the core or onset of the mental state to its surface or endpoint, with successive partitions undergoing continuous — or perhaps saltatory — specification over phases, as described in mental process but applicable to brain, implies a single "operation" or law that is repeated over a series of progressively more distinct sub-categories, supplanting the conventional idea of a variety of mechanisms acting at different sites.

A difficulty with the equivalence of part/whole synthesis and whole/part analysis, i.e. two-way transmission, is that microgenesis, like evolution, maturation and growth, is uni-directional, though a "relaxation" of part into whole, or an incomplete revival that exposes antecedent wholes prior to partition, would give the appearance of a whole, i.e. a wider or more inclusive category, as an outcome of incipient, attenuated or unrealized parts. The whole/part relation as it applies to the mind/brain problem is an alternative to causal resultants in the explanation of emergence. It is also the basis of novelty and its accentuation in creative thought. One can say that creativity entails the same qualitative whole/part transition as emergence, such that an account of one is an explanation of the other. However, the transition is not explicable on a causal basis, but rather as a propagation of concepts and their neural correlates through a variety of part-whole, e.g. metaphoric, relations, forming novel concepts by the revival of categories that prefigure unexpected outcomes, with conceptual growth by way of the merging of differing categories through shared predication.

2. On Coherence and Partition

For microgenesis, the object-field is the furthermost reach of mind into (as) the world, a sheet of mentality that traces back to the core of the observer's mind. Just as diversity at the surface of mind is assured by sensibility, so "persistence" at the base of the state is assured by the recurrence of proximal segments. The proximal includes instinctual drive, core beliefs and values, character and the unconscious self. These constructs maintain the stability and continuance of the individual, and support incipient acts and objects. Proximal or early segments are the scene of overlap of the occurrent and the oncoming. Initial phases in the present constrain, and are constrained by, comparable phases in the state that follows, segments that enfold preparatory segments of successors before the present state terminates (Fig. 2.1). The non-temporality of passage from earlier to later becomes temporal succession when the state actualizes as an epoch and a renewed cycle of iteration and replacement occurs.

As discussed, the transition over phases gives successive (virtual) contents that provide potential for sustained partitions with no existents until final actualization, but with a series of potentials sustained throughout the sequence. The virtual contents of a sub-category provide potential for further partition. Every phase of potential (category) leads to another potential (sub-category) until the process is complete, such that the microgenetic sequence of whole to part, or potential to actual, or category to sub-category, is a wave of potentialities guided by subjective aim, constrained by habit, recurrence and sensibility. Put differently, prior to final definiteness there is progressive delimitation as categories partition to sub-categories, with the phase-transition as a non-temporal or simultaneous becoming-into-being. The simultaneity is a succession that is not yet temporal, the final phase actualizing an epoch of serial partitions, at which point simultaneity discharges in serial order.

Simultaneity is an artifact of non-temporality, rather like a movie reel with a succession of simultaneous but sequential frames. We know that the progression over sub-categories is accompanied by increasing selectivity of (virtual) content in the continuum, because concealed segments actualize prematurely in pathological disorders. The study of symptoms in patients with focal brain damage reveals intervening phases that are otherwise opaque to introspection. This is why Whitehead's claim of immediate passage from potential to actual is not quite accurate. The transition from the simultaneity of non-temporality to the serial order of actuality is immediate on termination of the state, which consists of a sequence of phases that do not actually exist until the series achieves one epoch or cycle of existence.

To sum up: early phases lack existence, while later ones undergo individuation of categories to final partition. Unimpeded transition of non-temporal categories conforms to speculations as to the simultaneity or timelessness of the unconscious. The hypothesis of micro-temporal phases or successive whole-part transitions would remain purely speculative if not for the clinical evidence of content-specification over the transition. Ordinarily, the hierarchy of categories and sub-categories is a continuously refined potentiality that, through the subjective aim, individuates a final outcome unless disruption at some point in the whole-part sequence uncovers submerged phases when the transition, as well as the mode of transit, allows content to become actual as a pathological symptom.

The genesis of an epoch begins with the revival of its ground, while coherence at the terminus, e.g. oneness or unity in the diversity of the perceptual world, is owed to the commonalty of origin or the diachronic nature of specification that, on completion, gives the momentary state. The world before us seems unified even in change, in part because the object-field, as in a dream, is a conspiracy of the senses — visual, auditory, tactile, etc. — which develop in parallel out of the self, partly because repeated whole-part shifts compress diversity through repeated specification, allowing increasing coherence at multiple points, and partly because the causal progression of the world inferred from its appearance in perception combines with endogenous meaning-relations to give direction and purpose to the multiplicity of external events.

The perceived coherence of the world, in which the non-randomness of innumerable events depends on the presumption of their causal inheritance, consists in its formative history and sensory adaptation. Unlike dream, in which seeming randomness is integrated by meaning, e.g. the narrative of interpretation, in wakefulness the inference of causality makes events intelligible. We do not look for meaning in the external world, only cause and effect, while we explain dream by meaning-relations, not causation. Indeed, in dream, a putative cause is not present and can only be inferred, e.g. an ascent of stairs as a substitute for sexual contact. The cause is inferentially or metaphorically present, while the effect is presumed to be a symbolic representation of the cause, actually, a replacement based on relations of meaning (as well as shape, size, etc.). Imagination, which is part dream, part perception, approaches causal explanation when it approximates rationality, i.e. is superficial in mind and, at a depth, enlists meaning as an explanation when it employs syncretic, animistic or paralogical thought.

It is likely that each phase resolves discrepant possibilities within and across parallel streams, with conflicts (ordinarily) resolved in a commonality of need and purpose filtered through a relatively uniform sensibility. The underpinning infuses partitions with an allocation of feeling to every segment, that is, to the potentiality of the segment and the incipient contents. Feeling energizes categories and binds disparate elements, specifying drive into desire, and continuing as the value that accompanies and distributes into every object. The external world, which is the destination of the waking mind/brain state, delimits the epoch to an occasion of sensibility with one or another segment prominent, e.g. self, thought, perception, no less in human mind than in the genesis and recurrence of a flower.

The individuation of one or several items from a category — intermediate or final — entails a competition among possibilities that can be interpreted as a form of conflict. The item that is selected leaves others unborn, at times creating a certain tension between the path not chosen and that which is selected. This is more intense at early phases that condition the formative direction of the state, but occurs later as well. The early is close to personality, the later, to act and object. Thus, discord of core values at early phases precedes object- and word-choice at later ones. With unconscious conflict at the origin, drive may partition to desires that are unhealthy or self-destructive. Competing needs, wants and beliefs come into play early, while final act or word selection, which is closer to objectivity and adaptation, entails (a feeling of) conscious choice rather than unconscious conflict. Unconscious conflict becomes conscious choice when there is dissonance within a later category. Early options follow the "logic" of meaning and symbolism; later ones relate to a logic of reason closer to objects and amenable to causal explication. One path dominates, whether need trumps desire or the reverse. Conflicts arise when an outcome that adapts to immediate sensibility or the discharge of a need that is unopposed is harmful over the long term. For example, a drive may lead to destructive outcomes or inappropriate desires, but later phases of rational thought or competing desires closer to objectivity may lead to tension, as one drive or desire struggles for dominance. Early instigation or motivation is often implicit, later it may be explicit. Since conflicts are prior to adaptation, values that are irreconcilable with actions, except in psychoanalytic interpretation, are not open to causal explication.

3. Novelty and Change

In ordinary language, something is novel if it, or the context in which it occurs, has not occurred before. The usual definition of novelty as something new, interesting or unusual is not particularly helpful, for even if we recognize that it defers an account of newness or the profundity of a high order of originality, or the relation to change, or beauty in artistic creativity, novelty applies equally to a sonnet of Shakespeare as to scratching one's initials on a tree. There is no algorithm that goes from one level of novelty to another save for extrinsic features — intricacy, rarity, degree of difficulty — or the inability of others to conceptualize or replicate a certain level of complexity.

If an object is not considered in isolation from its spatial and temporal context, say the momentary state of the world, or temporal relations to antecedent and consequent occurrences, or conditions internal and external, it is clear that nothing is ever the same. In spite of the stability of cyclical (if not linear) time—seasons come and go, the weather is never the same, the universe moves on—so if things are viewed in relation to the state of the external world novelty appears to be continuous and universal. Change is so persistent and sweeping that we cannot even step in the same river once! Sameness is similarity by virtue of belonging to a common category, whether an object, a person or a sunny day. From this standpoint, a thing is both the same and different from all other prior or subsequent manifestations.

On the other hand, a chair at this moment and five minutes earlier appears unchanged, though everything around the chair, and within it, is different even if the difference is scarcely if at all noticed. But this simple contextual account of the career of a chair is not an interesting approach to novelty, though it subscribes to an evident solidity in relation to surrounding events and treats objects as part of a universal dynamic of physical change. Such a view has merit, but it does not address iterated, ongoing and intrinsic change in the object itself. More precisely, the ordinary account of change does not take into consideration the internal relations that make an object what it is and, in the case of organism, an increase in mentality in the course of evolution. The novelty that is here discussed, genuine novelty, is conceived as uniform, having the same basis in primitive organism as in human mind. Novelty is a constant, a universal, bound up with intrinsic properties of change and the inner nature of things, thus with replacement and continuance. Creativity, which increases over the evolutionary series, discussed below, is a somewhat different matter.

Novelty can be contrasted with repetition and/or predictability, but repeatability, as the recurrence of an epoch of change, is a foundational principle of process theory. What recurs is process and transition, not the content that develops in the transition.[25] The content may or may not be repeated, but

---

[25] A similar distinction clarifies the relation of pathology to maturational growth. The failure to find evidence that brain pathology exposes earlier phases in development, i.e. the regression hypothesis, led to the demise of this theory, when what is relevant is not the return of content, but an exposure of the process through which content is laid down.

regardless of what content actualizes, the process of actualization, that is, the pattern of transition through which things come into being, remains the same. The repeatability of states is the recurrence of a process, not an exact repetition and not with the same content, even if it appears identical, as in repeating a word or focusing on an object. Exact repetition is not a legitimate claim of any theory, causal or processual. Causality is a linear, externalist model of change, which postulates that every effect has a cause, and every cause has an effect, but it is largely silent on how things change. The instigation of change and its outcome are the pillars of causal theory, but what is left out is actual change.

Microgenesis is a recurrence theory with the opposite problem, how things remain the same, with an obligation to reconcile novelty and replication, or explain how replication is even possible in a world of universal flux. Genuine novelty is not a change in sensibility or in the internal state of an entity or organism; rather, it occurs in spite of the grip of sensibility on one side, and rigid habit on the other. Habit refers to the obvious but trivial patterns of regularity in behavior, such as a morning coffee or an afternoon nap, but more importantly, the unconscious patterns that lay down character and personality, along with those determinants of becoming that are ingrained influences or well-traveled paths in actualization.

Insofar as habit is a sign of recurrence, it reinforces replication theory, but it is also a problem for novelty. The more habitual an act, the less novel it would seem to be. Yet it is an important principle that novelty is not in the product but in the transition to that product, even if the latter does not seem to exhibit novelty. Whether a pattern of gait, a skill or a compulsion, every act of cognition, just to become what it is, regardless of what that is, and no matter how habitual, undergoes a process in which novelty is fundamental. Regardless of whether an outcome is the "same", which refers to its membership in, or representation of, a category, intrinsic novelty is an obligatory feature of the process through which habit is implemented.

The question then becomes: what is genuine novelty? To begin with, novelty depends on the potential of categories to evoke members as not-yet-actualized subordinates. Prior to actuality, categorical members are inchoate, insubstantial and non-particulate. An item in a category is itself a category, incipient, enmeshed in a bed of non-intentional meaning-relations, some close to the target, other distant, some essential to elicitation, others possible, improbable and/or implicit, including analogy, metaphor and related phenomena. The item arises in a multitude of possible relations, as a wave in the ocean or a sapling in the soil. Ordinarily, when we perceive or name an object, e.g. a chair, we can summon up a host of relations, proximate items such as rhymes to the word, or similar chairs, perhaps other pieces of furniture, our own or those of others, then to thrones, kings, dynasties. The spread of "associations" is open-ended, eventually including the sum of our experience linked to the item, however tenuously. We think this process is an exercise in associative memory applied to an actualized word or object. However, the microgenetic idea is that all present and historical relations are active prior to the realization of the word or object, and that to think of them afterward is to revive latent experiences (as Proust does) that make up the potential for the object prior to its selection. The point is that an elaboration on a word or object is not an association made on a second (or third, or fourth) pass, but a revival of bypassed or traversed relations from which the original object was selected.

Thus, with partial resolution, the item-to-be, weakly demarcated from its neighbors, is embedded in an inconceivably rich lattice of actual and possible relations. Even if we restrict the process to a narrow category, such as "dogs", the members of the category include all types of dogs, including boundary items, e.g. foxes, and not only instances of these animals, but extinct and/or ancestral forms, dogs of different gender, age, color, temperament, use, habitat, not to mention other animals of similar size and shape, i.e. spatial relations. Even restricted to a single dog, the animal is not a thing but a category that subsumes its varied manifestations at different times, ages, moods, color, health, and so on. Apart from its qualities, there is no such thing as a dog, whether a supra- or sub-ordinate entity, except as a category that includes a particular dog of which each manifestation is an instance.

A category may appear bounded but its membership is limitless. All relations are ingredient in any exemplar; this is most apparent at intermediate phases, when the elicitation has not reached a final outcome. In each transition, implicit relations differ in their application to the target as it specifies. The goal of specification is to realize a particular from a matrix of possibilities. Habit guides the process and sensibility adapts it to some subset of external conditions, assuring the item does not actualize prematurely and evoke an implausible train of possibilities derailing the intentional aim. This derailment, by the way, which a variety of operations attempts to prevent, is the key to creative thought.

It should also be clear that perceiving a dog is similar to exercising a habit, in that each perception, like every habitual act, individuates a novel background whether or not the act or object is the same as before. Conversely, a departure from habit is comparable to a shift in perceptual interest. Thus, while brushing one's teeth or drinking a cup of coffee in the morning may be habitual, the events are not merely repetitive but develop as similar members of a category. With habit, the constraints on resolution are internal. In perception, constraints are external. In both, constraints parse category-item shifts and restrict relations to relevant targets, with the relational quality of the derivation comparable in perception and other acts of thought.

The elicitation of sub-categories is, in some respects, a successive decomposition in the passage from the more general to the more restrictive, though each sub-category is essentially without limits. The category of animals or insects, which appears wider than that of dogs, is a comparison of one reservoir of enormous virtual capacity to another. Since category members have to be specified anew each instance, each phase of passage must be sampled in an evocation of the ensuing one.[26] The resolution through a traveling wave of whole-to-part shifts that is essentially infinite is the source of intrinsic novelty even if, from an external point of view, the

---

[26] Borges touches on this phenomenon is his story of Funes, whose limitless memory resulted in the recall of every hair at every moment in the mane of every horse in a galloping herd. A horse is a category of all instances of momentary existence, just as a tree remains the "same" over seasonal and other changes.

final item seems more or less inexorable or is a repetition of its antecedent. Each transition or becoming individuates a network of relations that may be similar but is never quite the same. *In sum, we can say that intrinsic novelty in every act of becoming-into-being, realized to a varying extent in every entity over sets of whole/part or category/member transforms, develops in a relational web of potentiality or possibility irrespective of how densely it is accessed or how narrowly it is implemented.*

In this light, a continuum of becoming over a modular epoch offers ample — indeed, obligatory — opportunities for the manifestation of novelty at every phase. Categories do not contain fixed items but specify sub-categories, with actuality postponed until the final individuation. Every category, including the final one, has countless relations to other members, to itself at different moments, and to a multitude of possible instantiations, regardless of progressive delimitation. The initial categorical prime and successive partitions have near-inexhaustible potentiality. The fact that deviance in final specification is unusual in normal individuals, e.g. naming a chair as a chair, can be attributed to the relative fixity of the drive that empowers the becoming, the need-based origins of desire (intentional aim), the channeling of habitual pathways, the elimination of maladaptive alternatives and the "causal influx" of sensibility. Once the hidden sequence of categories that mediate the transmission from onset to finality is uncovered, in spite of limits on variation by need and habit, or on deviance by sensibility, we see that novelty even with predictability is as inevitable as recurrence.

The potential for multiple instantiations of a category-member is essentially without limits. The *whole* of the category is the embrace of incipient multiplicity. As discussed, an item once individuated is still a category, even with diminution of potential as other possibilities are eliminated. However, in addition to a myriad number of "positive" (competing or contributing) relations, there is a host of "negative" (opposing or improbable) relations. An example of the latter would be all non-doglike things in the world, from a subtle distinction to an obvious difference. To say an animal is a dog is to imply it is not a cat, a bear or a bee, as well as to imply it has four legs, is a mammal, does not have a beak, feathers, scales or fly, does not live in water or on the moon, and so on. If you eliminate all the weeds in a garden so a flower can bloom, in what sense does the absence of weeds *cause* the growth of the flower? It is the *reason* why the flower blooms, but is it the cause?

If an item is evoked by inhibition of other members, what those members are depends on the phase that is active. One could suppose that initially the antecedents of the word or object dog arise in the suppression of all other words and objects. Thus, it is not only neighboring members that are suppressed but also all unrelated categories. An object is defined as much as by what it is as by what it is not. A figure does not exist without a ground, an object without the world around it, a word without an implicit lexicon. This *via negativa* provides a backdrop of un-actualized contents essential to the arousal of any given item. In the transition, sub-categories appear *in lieu* of particulars as substrates for the final partition. The play of alternatives at each phase, from categorical prime to outcome, even if it does not appear to be novel, exhibits novelty in the arousal of items over the relational series.

As in the above example, to name an object or say a word, e.g. chair, requires the drive-category to activate a mental state that passes to object- and lexical-concepts, zeroes-in on the sub-category, e.g. furniture, goes on to the desired word-frame, then the proper speech sounds in correct order, finally the articulatory apparatus. At each phase, multiple alternatives come into play. We can describe the sequence because it is exposed in the verbal performance of patients with focal brain damage. The complexity and relational quality of these phases, implicit in the final word, explains why each repetition must differ from its predecessor as to what is ingredient in the transition of categories, as well as competing possibilities, ease of transmission, purpose and so on. The outcome of derivation is always uncertain, always novel, whether for the same item or for those unforeseen, whether overt or concealed, whether evident at onset or subsequent phases.

The conventional account of word production or object perception is so banal one wonders why it is not only believed but constitutes the dominant theory of such phenomena:

namely, that a word is accessed directly from a mental lexicon and an object is assembled from its features. While ancillary contacts and intervening stages are acknowledged, e.g. relation to a semantic store for words, relation to spatial features of the environment for objects, a word in a store is presumed unchanged in its transfer to conscious production, while an object, once assembled, is projected into external space. The philosopher Mario Bunge dubbed this the Lego theory of the mind. In thinking about these relations, consider the proposal by Eccles (1970) that "higher functions" should be explained on the basis of field effects rather than, as is the practice, by the extrapolation of a synaptic model of neuronal transmission to the interaction of mental components.

On the microgenetic account, every act and object passes through successive fields or wave fronts, which consist of distributed neural configurations that are determined by millions, if not billions, of synaptic connections of varying strength and relevance. Moreover, it is not only the active synaptic connections that play a role in shaping the configuration, whether excitatory or (more importantly) inhibitory, but the dormant ones as well. What is inactive is pertinent to what is active, especially to what is suppressed. The idea that a word or object depends on an enormous multitude of synapses that establish the pattern of configurations at successive phases in transition, including the latency or suppression of an infinite array of competing possibilities, e.g. aroused, suppressed, dormant, and those of all other behaviors that could be entrained, points to a near-incomprehensible complexity and all but guarantees the impossibility of exact replication.

Chapter 7

Creativity

The creative comes unbidden

A brief review of some interpretations of creative thought led to a discussion of process theory and the relation of causation to recurrence, with novelty a universal of change and change a recurrent becoming-into-being. The category implemented in a final outcome constitutes the being of an entity, while the relational process of becoming, i.e. as a derivation of one or many categories, is the basis of novelty. Given this formulation, we are now in a position to tackle the nature of creativity from the standpoint of an intrinsic theory of change.

The most obvious locus of creativity, the outcome or product of thinking, is the basis for a judgment of the originality and depth of the work and an estimation of its value. The mental process underlying creativity has not been an active area of research in psychology for several reasons. To begin with, the process of creation is mysterious and studies of the thought process have not been able to elucidate the inner nature of thinking even at a rudimentary level, not to mention understanding the creativity of gifted individuals or autistic prodigies; secondly, the mind/brain process that lays down the product is obscure and therefore infrequently studied, apart from computational models and imaging studies that purport to show correlations of, say, musical ability with some portion of the brain; and finally, because the tools or methods of study are lacking.

Among the studies that have been done, that of Jackendoff and Lerdahl (1983) on the relation of music to language stands out in the attempt to map aspects of music to a model of

generative grammar, but the comparison is weakened by problems in linguistic theory, uncertainty if the model has psychological value or is purely formal, the absence of semantics in
music, and the failure to deal with brain and creativity (see
Levitan, 2007). The work is less an account of giftedness in
music than an application, to music, of a particular linguistic
theory.

From a psychological standpoint, discussions of the relation
of music and language going back to Darwin and Wagner
suggest that music is more fundamental.[27] Wagner thought so;
Darwin was non-committal (Kivy, personal communication).[28]
In my view, a series of kinetic melodies from the breath or tonal
group through the "speech melody" and prosodic contour to
the fine sequence of articulation is the substrate of language
production, but this rhythmic structure, which is certainly in
place in the brain prior to language and music, was initially
related to the sequence of phases in the unfolding of an action,
from postural or axial systems to fine distal motility. Music and
language exploit this structure.[29] The series of rhythmic layers
involves successive partitions of an oscillator for walking,
derived into limb movements. Similarly, the respiratory
rhythm that underlies or "pre-programs" speech and song
develops, in language production, over the same partitions. In
music, there is a progression from drum beats and dance—the
hypnotic repetition of primitive music—to chants and the
steady cadences of march to a more refined rhythmic or
melodic structure, as well as feeling, at all levels in mind/brain.
It is no coincidence that it is difficult to abstain from moving or
tapping one's foot when listening to the repetitious beat of
popular music, since music develops over the same system as
early stages in action and instinctual drive.

[27] See the collection in Arbib (2013) for papers on the evolution of music,
language and feeling in relation to brain.
[28] See Patel (2008) for an illuminating if inconclusive review of studies on the
evolution of language and music, as well as other work in the neuroscience
of music.
[29] Rhythmic structures in the derivation of action were described by Bernstein
(1967), and in speech by Martin (1972).

In sum, a sequence of oscillatory levels from archaic to recent in forebrain evolution is presumed to support song, music and speech, along with their affective tonalities. This sequence may represent a fundamental frequency that specifies through a harmonic structure initially dedicated to action.

Another approach to the creative use of language, scholarly but somewhat anecdotal and without a guiding theory, is illustrated by the study of Lowes (1927) on the experiential precursors of the *Kubla Khan* of Coleridge. Concepts similar to pregnancy were employed (conception, gestation and parturition), or elsewhere, ingestion, incubation and inspiration (see also Koestler, 1964). Basically, the idea is that a good deal of experience, learning and preparation are necessary for creative work. The interval of absorption is accompanied by an unconscious organization and integration (see below) that reaches a boiling point on an occasion of inspiration, then followed by the labor of composition. This approach raises the important question of how a creative work develops or is "put together" in the mind. I would claim that the ingredients of a creative work do not accumulate to a thematic whole, for there is no procedure or algorithm that could unconsciously sort through the multiplicity of data to arrive at a coherent idea. Rather, the idea, even if embryonic,[30] searches for instantiations in study and personal experience through a process in which irrelevant data are suppressed in favor of those which support or nourish the forming concept. In a word, the concept is unpacked from inside-out, enlarging through a fractal-like individuation, not addition.

The linguistic model of music generation is an account of process irrespective of content, as is microgenesis, while the fascinating but inconclusive expedition by Lowes into the life of Coleridge attempts to relate the content of experience to a literary work. As noted, the problem remains why this or that experience is selected unless, as argued, the concept specifies the data appropriate to its fulfillment. The anecdotal quality of literary interpretation is not unlike psychoanalytic explorations of literature or art (e.g. Kris, 1962), which depend heavily on

---

[30]   Bergson wrote of his main idea as a "contact."

the content of experience, often chosen according to some theoretical bias, whether aesthetic taste or oedipal conflict, with little attention to the formative process leading to satisfaction, inspiration, the "ascent" to consciousness, and the deliverance of the idea into reflective or creative thought.

Moreover, an interpretation of artistic work based on childhood conflict or events later in life does not separate the creative thinker from the pack of others with a comparable life history, a similar influence and exposure, or even those with a passion for some avenue of artistic expression or philosophical thought. Mahler and my Polish grandmother both sang folk songs of childhood when close to dying, but grandma, bless her, was no prodigy. Psychoanalysis is a formulaic and homuncular theory without a plausible model of thought development to account for the varieties of ordinary, pathological and creative cognition. Attempts at a theory by Rapaport, Schilder and others in Freudian thought, or Hillman in Jungian, have generally failed to influence the orthodoxy.

The first neuropsychological study of an artwork was probably Paul Schilder's interpretation of *Through the Looking Glass,* focusing on body-image alterations, but again, though Schilder was a prolific and revolutionary thinker who wrote papers on thought-development (Schilder, 1951), to my knowledge his work did not address the creative process. Most current psychological and philosophical models are static, descriptive and content-based, for example, an account of mental states in terms of imagery, propositional attitudes or mental statements, or general features such as openness and flexibility. Even if these features illustrate a mode of thought, a strategy or inventory of the conscious ingredients of a work, they are unhelpful without a theory of the processual aspects of content-generation or combination. Ideally, such an account should be applicable to all instances of thought and perception — creative, ordinary, eccentric, aberrant — as well as the relation of ideation to experience, or how the creative individual exploits or "selects" data from the enormity of even a brief experience, and the relation of an idea to the core beliefs, values and feelings behind it and beyond it, to the particularity of actualized content. The eccentricity of the creative mind can be uncovered even in the most casual remarks. Thus, most of us have heard bells toll the hour, but how many are capable of saying, as Coleridge did, the clock has gone mad; it has struck one 4 times.[31]

Koestler (1964) and Mehta (1963), among others, give many examples, in the prepared individual, of sudden insight or enlightenment, whether a spontaneous flash or an encounter with an idea or behavior from an unexpected source or in dream. This Eureka moment occurs as an immediate awareness of a novel idea, theme or solution, e.g. the well-known report by Poincaré of insight to a mathematical problem prior to its proof. The moment of inspiration may be brief and intense or recurrent with revival in composition. It may be triggered by some stimulus that allows a resolution of unconscious mentation to surface into consciousness, or for the individual to see a problem in an entirely different light, or the insertion of a needed ingredient that completes or integrates an ideational set. Possibly, the conceptual segregation of one line of thought clashes with another that overlaps in some respect, expanding the original category or forming a new one in which both concepts are enclosed. The outcome would be a transformation of the developing idea and its content to accommodate the intruder.

There are two main problems to consider; the unconscious development of the creative idea, and the moment of inspiration, which is usually not as frequent or dramatic as advertised. In many respects, this resembles the distinction of falling in love gradually, and falling in love at first sight, a *coup de foudre*. In my view, conceptual growth does not come about by the addition, combination or intersection of two otherwise unrelated ideas, or so-called lateral thinking, though this can give lively thought, wit and originality, but rather to "vertical" thinking, to an exploration of a concept, or an impulse to satisfaction of the central theme or idea (category). Conceptual growth results from a specification that propagates by predicative overlap to form a new category or incorporate

---

[31] There is a description of a similar exclamation by Gassendi in a transitional state (Janet, 1879).

neighboring or distant concepts. The original predicates expand to a concept related by nothing more than a single attribute.

1. Categories and Attributes

The attributes of a category can be enumerated, e.g. dogs are mammals, have four legs, a tail, etc., but ordinarily the category is largely unconscious, its attributes implicit or unspecified. Potential attributes such as loyal, vicious, sad, are not defining features, but are specific to members of the category. A virtual or unrealized attribute is a possibility equivalent to a category with the potential for a near-infinite number of members. For example, "tail" can be an attribute or a category, but as a category it calls up innumerable objects or properties other than dogs, not only subordinate features of a tail, e.g. short, long, wagging, but the tail of a kite or plane, the tail-end of a story, a woman's posterior, and if phonological relations apply, a tale, and so on, with all of the attributes associated with those objects. The potency of the attribute applies when it is implicit; after that, its power is weakened. More precisely, once stated, a metaphor or simile can be enjoyed as a creative product, e.g. Juliet is the sun, but its polyvalency and generative force in the unconscious is lost. Hemingway once remarked, to paraphrase, "I never talk in bed for I use up my best lines that way." Artists are notoriously secretive about works in progress, partly, I suspect, to avoid objectifying the idea, preferring to leave it inchoate and replete with possibility.

If the ingredients of an idea or theory lack a necessary coherence, the Eureka moment may change the perspective so that the problem or theme has a more harmonious relation to its constituents, or the coherence is retained from a different perspective. This is comparable to a move in grandmaster chess that alters the entire pattern of relations while maintaining unity and balance among the pieces. To re-play a game by Capablanca is to enjoy sustained creative growth; to play Alekhine is to feel inspiration in a sudden electric move. In blindfold chess, the master recalls the strategy, i.e. idea, then reconstructs the board in which the pieces are ingredient. Perhaps the elicitation of a move in relation to the pattern, with the opponent serving as the world that constrains the move—thought into action—the advance of the idea, its maintenance throughout the game, its relation to the pieces and the beauty of a perfect game, make high-level chess a model of creative thought.

In any case, a mode of metaphoric extension in which shared attributes give insight to, or reorganize, an earlier ideational or thematic structure is the likely basis of conceptual growth. When the idea reaches some point of fulfillment it can give rise to insight or inspiration. The concept, "triggered" by an inter-current stimulus or replete with virtual data, "bubbles up" with provocation. The implicit overlap supports the growth and/or resolution of the submerged idea or novel perspective, at times helping the idea achieve final coherence, realize an unconscious aim or affirm the truth or value of a belief. The inspired individual is usually certain of the truth of the idea, whether or not it is true, even (especially) if it is delusional, but it is doubtful that inspiration brings to consciousness the *recognition* of an erroneous or fallacious idea. Conviction is powerful for false beliefs, not for beliefs acknowledged to be false. The recognition that an idea is false would ordinarily coincide with the consciousness of another idea that, to the thinker, is true. The absolute conviction in the truth of an inspired idea must often entail the rejection, even if implicit, of a pre-existing concept assumed to be true. The immediacy of conscious discharge and the weight of the antecedent concept, when it is not stalled at a phase of choice or decision, may explain the certainty that is common in creative thought. It is fair to say that in most instances inspiration points to a certainty, not options to be considered.

The fact that many creative ideas, like Kekule's vision of snakes or Wagner's Prelude to *Das Rheingold*, occur in dream or a transitional state is consistent with the withdrawal from consciousness and reason to the imagination, or to unconscious and para- or pre-logical thought, as well as a metaphoric, animistic or syncretic mode of thinking. It is of interest that problem-solving evokes the propagation of thought by way of predication, a more preliminary phase of verbal imagery, i.e. inner speech (Vygotsky, 1987ed). The process is no doubt

partly or largely unconscious.[32] The idea may be experienced
directly in the unconscious of dream, in the transition to consciousness, or with an insight breaking into consciousness from
a presumed unconscious origin. The totality of the idea in a
simultaneous or spatial image directly transmitted to consciousness, without a pause for introspection, would account
for its intensity and suddenness, and the obscurity of its
origins. Wagner's experience is instructive, in part through his
account in *Mein Leben,* but more by an analysis of the Prelude.
Clearly, the prior composition of the Ring constitutes a
necessary preparation and a wish, conscious or not, to integrate
the complex whole of the cycle, as well as other attitudes and
personal experience, in a single musical idea.

Thus, the music begins with a slow undulating chord in the
bass, calling to mind the lower currents of the Rhine, continuing throughout the piece, which first partitions to a fifth,
then to livelier and more turbulent rhythms. The progression
suggests a fundamental frequency that individuates to
harmonics; for the listener, it evokes an image of arising from
the depths of this storied river to the waves at the surface, as
well as forecasting the continuum from the subterranean to the
celestial, from Nibelheim to Valhalla. The opening of the
curtain with the singing of the Rhine maidens brings into
public space, i.e. conscious perception, the privacy of unconscious process. The piece builds to a crescendo and bursts into
song, bringing to mind Wagner's views on the priority of music
in the evolution of speech. The blending of themes in a brief
introduction is extraordinary, regardless of the extent to which
Wagner was aware of the accomplishment. The origin of the
musical idea in a dream points to the lack of deliberation and
the unconscious work involved in the integration of so many
ideas.

Moreover, to anticipate commentary below, the central
evolutionary theme of the Ring—progression over levels and
the advance of higher forms—applies to stages in rhythmic
structure, to the transition from music to speech or depth to

---

[32]   Vygotsky cites the lines of Mandelshtam: I forgot the word that I wanted to
       say, and thought, unembodied, returns to the hall of shadows.

surface in the Rhine, to the development from archaic to recent in evolution and social order, e.g. the relation of Alberich to Wotan, and no doubt to other attitudes and experiences, such as overcoming a lowly birth or a virulent anti-Semitism, which also refer to a relation of lower to higher. The application of the theme to these and other phenomena illustrates a principle of metaphoric expansion or overlap of objects or concepts by way of shared features, while the relation of feature to concept, e.g. lower to the Rhine, to a prostitute as his mother, to Alberich and Jews, embodies the partition of wholes and their identi-fication by shared parts.

In my personal experience at various stages in the develop-ment of microgenetic theory, there have been occasions of sudden insight in which a critical idea came in the course of sustained concentration, or in a transitional state, as a vivid visual or autosymbolic image (Silberer, 1951) of the whole and its constituents. One example concerned the difficulty in mapping a dynamic theory of (pathological) language to the then static notions of brain anatomy. The idea of stages in language that develop over evolutionary formations and the relation of language pathology in children to that in adults, that is, the sweep of maturational change in the unfolding of language and its correspondence to morphology, came all at once as a spatial and to some extent pictorial vision of clarity, power and certainty. The more common experience is less dramatic, namely brief insights or small ideas akin to problem-solving in the course of composition that resolve unexpected dilemmas or uncertainties in the continuation of the work.

The intersection of two lines of thought, or the overlap of one with the other, giving a sudden insight or rethinking an unresolved problem, often with tension before arriving at a solution,[33] points to a central feature of the whole-part tran-sition, exemplified in the role of metaphor, simile, analogy and related phenomena. Metaphor is especially prominent in poetry, where properties of objects provide a bridge across concepts, or the parts (features) of a whole (object/category)

---

[33]   See Lewin (1948) for studies of this topic and the so-called Zeigarnik effect.

are extracted to form a novel category. What occurs in music is similar to what happens in literature. In Wordsworth, for example, metaphoric expansion or fusion appears in his depiction of solitude and loneliness as wandering lonely as a cloud, or his feeling of isolation in relation to a "host of golden daffodils", or the contrast of his melancholy with the joyfulness of flowers dancing in a breeze. The fusion of human emotion with that of a flower, of personal solitude with companionship — the solitary Wordsworth and a field of flowers — exchanges and collapses features of widely divergent categories. The mental operation involves the extraction and conflation of like features of disparate objects, such as solitude, which then, even if essential to composition, becomes a subject or topic in the poem.

Metaphor and its derivations are common in everyday language, a pernicious but productive example being the frozen metaphor of the brain as a computer. What distinguishes the poet is the originality of the bridging attributes and their function in the poem. One of my favorites is Philip Larkin's: "time is the echo of an axe within a wood." This captures the illusory quality of time as an echo, the instantaneity in the knife-edge, and the paradox of time as motion in a motionless state.[34] Whether metaphoric expansion occurs within an original or novel category, e.g. one that includes the loneliness of clouds and poets, currents in a river and troglodytes in a myth, what is central is that subject/ predicate or object/attribute relations, which are fundamental in the propagation of thought, illustrate the relation of parts to wholes in the growth of novel concepts.

Moreover, the occurrence of conceptual growth at unconscious phases conforms to the evolutionary principle that new growth occurs as branching from earlier stages, not as endpoints of specialization. In yet another stroke of genius, Wagner's representation of Siegfried as a higher level in evolution that arises from the potentiality of Nature is an

---

[34]   This recalls Aristotle's "time as the number of motion" or Plato's time as "the moving image of eternity", relating the illusion of time to the timelessness of time eternal or unending.

intuition of this principle. While the content of an idea provides a basis for the distinction of ordinary and creative thought, as well as grades of creativity from the unexceptional to genius, it does not explain the exercise of thought and imagination in the service of creative outcomes. The analysis to this point indicates that creativity depends on access to universal novelty, its complexity and sustained unity and then its magnification to an order higher than possible for most people.

The creative idea refers to a category of thought energized by feeling that accompanies constituents as possibilities that are ordinarily unconscious pending composition. The constituents manifest a relation to the originating concept such that each derives from, and in turn evokes, the potential of the under-lying category, which is revived on each occasion of compo-sition to provide a conceptual refuge from which items can arise: brush strokes, sentences, notes. The fragments of an artwork or the data of a scientific theory are not isolated bits of information, but configurations embedded in a spatial and temporal context, part-objects of a category that provides thematic structure to its partitions.

A world of experience stands behind a single phrase; an experiential history can be accessed in a poem or sonata. A great work has authenticity. It arises in relation to personality and character, as a more or less direct expression or as a compensatory effort. The work traces back to implicit beliefs. Microgenetic theory holds that mind is unity at the onset, but many believe there is duality, thus conflict, at the core, with good and evil the prime candidates. Creative work traces back to implicit knowledge and experiential history. A less profound idea does not tap the depth of the creator, but expresses a more superficial layer distinct from deeper belief. It is not only the idea that guides the work, but the force of a genuine per-sonality. The whole of the individual goes into the work—as in love—with an origin in feeling that arises in drive, passes through desire and enlivens objects with value. In this way, the theme of a book or symphony, i.e. what holds it together as more than a haphazard collection, so that its elements "fit" with an overarching idea, is that the idea and its ingredients trace to a genuine impulse of the heart, which corresponds to a derivation out of core categories that inform the discharge of each constituent. The guiding category is a source of unity and harmony, and also of the aesthetic of the work as a whole, with the position of each ingredient fully realized and actualizing the overall theme.

The proportionality that is seen or heard in an artwork or theory by observer and creator is the balance of novelty and coherence in relation to the scope of the category, the depth to which it is plumbed, the "rightness", felicity and functional role of each element, i.e. the conformance of elements to each other and their source in the category, and the originality of theme and implementation. *In a word, creativity samples the becoming of parts out of wholes, or the realization of the whole through the parts, or the maintenance of the whole in each part, with the category as theme to the parts that are selected.*

A further point is that the revival of the concept in each round of composition entails a return to a certain mood, a generalized feeling prior to individuation. For example, anxiety is a mood that becomes fear when an object specifies. The mood has a potential that can distribute into more precise affects. The ability to revive the idea through a mood allows particular feelings to facilitate the extraction of data in the course of composition. This ability is often felt to be a fragile and tenuous gift that is dependent (perhaps more in artistic than scientific creativity, but probably also in mathematical and philosophical thought) on the re-evocation of a mood and the distribution of its affective tonalities into the individuated data. This explains some unusual tendencies in artists, previously discussed. The goal is to arouse, or lapse into, a particular mood conducive to creative work, which diffuses into specific feelings that accompany constituents as they develop. Probably, the primary need serviced by the mood is a sustained relaxation that promotes inwardness, concentration and imaginative flow. The relaxation is to reduce conscious focus and, along with the mood, to retreat from perception to the inner life, while concentration is not to select but to release, and avoid distraction.

Personally, my writing "flows" better near water, perhaps as a symbol of unconscious thought, or because an ocean or pool relates to my sense of cognition as a wave-like process. Many writers prefer privacy in a social milieu rather than in solitude, e.g. Sartre, who wrote in a café. The setting, possibly including a ritual, is often essential for writing to proceed. The need to recapture the mood prior to specification, the affective tonalities to which it gives rise, and the deliverance of ingredients from the revived category can itself be an obstacle to overcome and a source of anxiety. Most creative work unfolds over a lengthy period, with a need for the mood to recur over many occasions. There is no guarantee this will occur, especially in modern life, with so many distractions to impede the return of a specific feeling. Seclusion came naturally to the great men of the past without cell phones, internet or ease of travel, but nowadays, with isolation sought-after and self-imposed, it is a wonder that a lengthy and creative work of a high order is even attempted.

2. Love and Creation

An example of an analogy that advances the argument and points to the role of feeling in the creative act is that between creativity and love.[35] The parallels are striking. Most people fall in love gradually, and at some point realize that a lover, an acquaintance or friend has become a beloved. It is important to "get to know" someone in different circumstances, and to experience one's own reactions, before love can be felt as genuine and commitment is given. Love can be obsessive, even sacrificial, but preoccupation with the creative idea can also border on obsession. Given the irrational behavior of lovers, and the sacrifice of artists and scientists who devote themselves wholly to their work, it is understandable that madness has been associated with both love and genius.

As with falling in love, creative ideas take time to develop, and as the idea develops, the individual becomes more deeply committed. At first the concept, e.g. a work, a beloved, is vaguely sensed, embryonic, a tendency, an interest, a problem. It may not be apprehended or recognized as significant before

---

[35] As an aside, see Hofstadter (1997ed) on the love affair as a work of art.

it reaches a point where the developing content or feeling justifies further engagement. Artistic or scientific creativity, like gradually falling in love, fulfills a predisposition or consolidates a line of thought. In both, there is a period of learning, a topic, a method or approach; in love, a growing familiarity. The *predisposition* narrows down to the category of potential-beloved; the *presupposition* narrows down the category of thought. The choice of a beloved and the expression of an idea both show a transition from inclination to commitment, from tendency to formulation, from need to expression.

Concept formation is variable, at times spontaneous, e.g. what to take on a picnic, or it may require days, months or years. The gradual and unconscious development of the concept in love, art and science, when it arrives at some point of relative maturity, may eventuate in a more or less sudden realization of the content, and of its significance and power, namely that one is in love or at the threshold of an important artistic or scientific breakthrough. The process that leads to inspiration is analogous to falling in love at first sight. Both require a preparatory phase, the desire for a salient object, immersion in desire, study or technique, and the creation of a set that aids the artist or scientist to recognize the beauty or truth of the idea, and for the lover to fall in love at first sight. Like the sudden insight to an idea, the beloved is recognized the moment he or she is first seen. Given the similarity, it is not surprising that genuine love at first sight is as infrequent as inspiration.

The analogy is compelling and implies that both phenomena involve a common process. Creative thought is a process of conceptual growth largely in the realm of ideas; falling in love is a process of conceptual growth largely in the sphere of feeling. Science involves concepts seemingly barren of feeling; love involves concepts seemingly barren of thought. Art is an expression of conceptual-feeling, intermediate between an arid concept and a torrid feeling, between reason and imagination.

The analogy of creativity and love introduces the role of feeling in the creative process. Though we think of science or philosophy as unrelated to feeling, there is an affective tonality in every concept, and a conceptual frame for every feeling. The affective tonality is a residue of feeling or process, while the conceptual frame is the equivalent of category as substance. The process that deposits a substance and the feeling that propels a category are both examples of becoming-into-being. While the affective quality of scientific concepts is subdued, it is felt as interest, value, motivation and the drive to completion. On the other hand, the conceptual aspect of love refers to the category of the beloved in which feeling is invested. Conceptual immersion in the artist or scientist may, in the case of the lover, become all-encompassing—a codependence or identification of creator and lover ensnared by objects of their own creation.

In sum, the conceptual-aspect of the feeling of love is the category of the beloved; the feeling-aspect of a work of science is the intensity of the unconscious strategy, its value, the struggle and the pleasure of discovery. In art, the concept is evident in the artwork; feeling is evident in emotions conveyed to an observer. Art uniquely evokes the feeling that is concealed in scientific thought, and the concept that is concealed in love.

3. Objections to the Analogy

Features of a gradual love that are not apparent in creativity can also shed light on the creative process. For example, one objection arises in the natural tendency to think of love as beginning with an encounter of autonomous individuals. The future-beloved comes from outside, unlike artistic creativity, which is self-generated. However, if one shifts the paradigm of external relations and superficial bonds to a conception of the beloved as an actualization of the lover's need and longing, not a mere addition or coming-together but a creation of each by the other, the aptness of the comparison will be obvious. The lover creates the beloved as an embodiment of the satisfaction of need and desire. For the lover, the beloved conforms to or fulfills the drive to complementarity in the self-concept. In most people, this is occasioned not only by obvious gender differences relating to functional morphology and temperament, but to the satisfaction, by the beloved, of a felt incompleteness.

Another difficulty is the need for reciprocity. Unless the creative individual is motivated solely by the desire for fame and approval, financial reward or celebrity, in which case the work is unlikely to be of a high order, the need to express a creative idea or the pressure of the idea to actualize is paramount. Ambition and the hope for success figure in most people, creative or not, but in the truly gifted the satisfaction of personal or impersonal need — as Bach put it, to create for the glory of god — provides reciprocity comparable to love, e.g. in purpose, enrichment and self-fulfillment. Artists in the past, and some moderns, e.g. Yeats, write for the ideal and the pleasure of a (female) muse. Kant made this point explicit in saying that philosophy was his mistress. The common replacement of love by work, or the reverse, attests to this phenomenon.

I think the attribution of creativity to divine intervention, outdated in moderns, might be one explanation for the superiority of the old masters. To create for an ideal, for deity or someone imagined, or to have in mind the great works of the past and (however whimsical, the concept may seem) the approval of the dead, ignoring the fickleness of crowds and evanescent taste, aiming at the highest, dissatisfied with the inferior, is necessary for the best of creative work.

One characteristic of love that seems alien to creativity is the common belief that the meeting of lovers was fated, starcrossed, or influenced by heavenly design. This belief has special resonance in some countries, such as India, where marriages are arranged or engagements cancelled according to the propitiousness of omens, tea leaves, horoscopes and astrological signs. Perhaps in cultures where love is secondary, fate does not play so great a role, but it is amusing, in modern life, to see how common the belief in fate is, even when the initial meeting is a blind date, or at a bar or on the internet. The felt implausibility in this vast universe of meeting one's soul-mate accounts for the belief that fate intervenes in the affairs of love. *In love, fate replaces luck or coincidence. In science, luck or serendipity replaces fate.* When lovers speak of fate there is an insinuation of romance, in helplessness and lack of will. Creativity is not noticeable, nor is personal accomplishment. Conversely, it sounds odd to speak of an artistic or scientific work as fated, even if the individual quietly believes this to be true. Self-aware geniuses may think they are destined to create great works. Oscar Wilde wrote famously that he put his genius into his life and only his talent into his work, which implies that except for hedonic pursuits, he felt destined to do greater things. On a less grandiose scale, the artist or scientist feels a self-author, even if the growth of the idea is largely unconscious, or even with the feeling of being a vehicle for inspired creation.

The difference in attitude also owes to the fact that creativity is conceived as an individual endeavor while love requires two minds in unison. Unlike genuine creativity, the need for the beloved implies that love is collaboration, a distinction that melts away if one takes the view that the other is a self-creation. In science or art, composition is recurrent, whether for a single work or ensuing ones. Once finished, the process of creation begins again to fulfill striving and creative energy. In contrast, while there are those for whom seduction is an art form that is sated on conquest, for most, having a beloved is an end in itself. One does not ordinarily go from one *great love* to another as a writer goes from one novel to the next. In art, a completed work is a temporary respite; in a great love, it is a final satisfaction. Yet an argument can be made that no matter how intense the love, it must be tended as a rare flower, continuously renewed, re-created as it were, as in the sustained composition of a new work.

4. Idealization and Authenticity

Essential to love is a process of idealization, e.g. he is the most attractive, gentle and loving of men; she is the most beautiful, intelligent and caring of women. In the course of falling in love, the beloved recedes from the world of fact to an image in the mind, a conscious or unconscious ideal. The attributes of the beloved form a category in which the beloved is beyond compare, with unique attributes that exclude all others.[36] Coherence

---

[36] Here the concern is with the formation of unconscious ideals, not models of simplicity with explanatory power. The account is closer to an Aristotelian approach, in which irrelevant attributes fall away with those left becoming ideals.

is achieved in the delimitation to the beloved of idealized qualities or an exclusivity of attributes, which are no less ideal than — indeed, they represent — the person as a whole. Even in instances where, to a spectator, the beloved seems ordinary, deficient or infirm, imperfections, if not overlooked, can become a source of compassionate loving that heightens the uniqueness and rarity of attributes the lover admires. On the other hand, some would say the qualities of the beloved, along with faults and inadequacies, should be appraised in an objective manner as an acceptance of one's partner in a love that is mature, not based on fantasy, since idealization is irrational and predisposes to disappointment should the ideal shatter. When this occurs, the ideal, which is largely unconscious, objectifies as hard truth, and the beloved leaves the imagination to return to a world of indifferent fact.

When the attributes of a beloved form a category, the subject becomes an exemplar of the qualities selected. That is, the beloved is no longer a subject to which the qualities are related; instead, the qualities form a category in which the beloved is the sole instance, actually a feature of the category, say the categorical prime of handsome or loving men. In idealization, other attributes fade away, with those left, and the person to whom they belong, perceived as unique and without compare, justified or not, approaching a kind of perfection. This may take the form: s/he is the most loving person in the world whose qualities or character perfectly fit the lover's need. It may be that the lover, when honest, will admit to the shortcomings of the beloved, but the force of the ideal comes not from conscious description but from its unconscious home. When the unconscious category surfaces, the subjectivity of love gives way to an objectivity in which judgment, not idealization, is the deciding factor.

There is a moral dimension in love, e.g. kindness, fidelity, which is less pronounced in art and science though they occur indirectly as a conflict for others (e.g. Heidegger's Nazism, Wagner's anti-Semitism), or as a conflict for the creator, e.g. Oppenheimer and the nuclear bomb. We tend to separate the life and character of artists and scientists from their work, such that what is problematic in or for artists is essential to love. The disconnect of character and work, or the disinterest of the observer in the character of the artist—in spite of, as shown in Wagner, the disguised roots of character in the art—presumes that genius is independent and radical, and not bound by propriety. This differs from love, in which attributes of character are a primary source of affection. In love, the ideal is authenticity. In art, it is truth and beauty. In love, a subjective ideal accompanies conviction in authenticity of feeling, which is ordinarily not in need of, indeed, is often resistant to, verification. Art is judged and validated; love seeks only affirmation. These differences are instructive, in that both love and creativity depend on whole-part relations, subjectivity, unconscious growth and an ideal, with the unlikeness serving to emphasize the process in common.

In artistic or scientific thought, a concept or category is delimited to the relevant object—topic, problem—which is also idealized, for example, the perfection or beauty of a theory or artwork. A profound idea in science, literature, philosophy, that approximates an ideal, comes close to perfection. A work with harmony in its elements, regardless of content, can be recognized, after Keats, as beauty in truth. An artwork with content that is disturbing, even repellent—the vision of hell in Bosch, in Beksinski or in Goya's dark paintings—may possess a certain beauty in the depiction of its theme.

The necessity of ingredients, the absence of trivial or adventitious content and, most important, the conveyance to the observer of a scene or narrative of power and a mind of ingenuity, creates beauty out of what is ordinary or disturbing. When the ideal represents the aim of creative work, whether or not it is pleasing, the content can be said to be truthful and authentic. The idea aims to exemplify the ideal to the extent it is approximated in composition.

5. Relation to Novelty

To an intermittent and varying degree, creativity samples the novelty that is the universal nature of change. Creativity is generally conceived as a feature of human mind. It is not only persons of exceptional talent who are creative; all or most people exhibit some creativity, whether in speech, improvised behavior or deviation from habit. Most higher mammals, even birds, some would say insects as well, find innovative solutions to unexpected problems. If we consider the human mind/brain state, the sampling accentuates the process of novelty as a spatiotemporal locus in mind; it transforms the concealed uniformity to an event. Novelty is uniform and constant, but in the mind/brain state, attributes at different phases can take on greater or lesser emphasis. Heightened novelty is creativity; lessened novelty, or a lack of emphasis on novel change, is habit. Like time, change proceeds irrespective of what is changing. Creativity settles at a phase of novel change and, according to the phase, exploits the process in creative thought. Gifted individuals tap into and elaborate features of novelty that, because they are unconscious and uniform, have limited availability to ordinary mind.

Creativity accesses novelty midway in the transition from core mind and experiential memory to conscious perception. The critical role of memory in (creative) thought is subsumed in imagery. Deviation to creative thought is coincident with self and imagery. A phase prior to what evolves to the visual and verbal imagination, or a phase that transits one of imagery *en route* to perceptual immediacy, is active in animal and human cognition in mediating a coping or adaptive strategy, but does not have creative potential. At a later phase of conscious perception, novelty is external and attributed to the causal progression of the world. To dwell at an intermediate phase of ideation—unconscious imagery and introspection—allows a category of thought to partition inwardly, organically and in a coherent manner. Recurrence to an intermediate phase nurtures the growth of the idea. The ability to tap this phase spontaneously or unconsciously over time, in passive release or intense concentration, is the gift of the creator.

In some artists, the inherent tendency to unconscious and organic growth is not enough left alone; rather, life is to be dedicated to facilitating a state of creativity. The mystical poet Hölderlin wrote of the need for risk, to walk the rim of an abyss, i.e. the depth of unconscious mind. The creator samples early layers in thought but returns, while some, like Hölderlin, fall in and cannot be rescued. The common association of artistic creativity with psychopathology, drugs or alcohol may represent an effort to enhance novelty, or the focus on sub-surface cognition may accompany or induce psychopathology. There is a greater ease of access to sub-surface phases that are figuratively "blocked" to conventional thought. It may be that a certain genetic predisposition—perhaps one that predisposes to psychopathology—is not for a specific talent or skill but for a facilitation or reduced impedance to a withdrawal to pre-terminal phases. Certainly, eccentricities in creators and the tendency for psychopathology appear to reflect a bias to the irrational roots of the creative. If this is not obvious in the creator, it may appear in full bloom in offspring, e.g. the schizo-phrenic daughter of James Joyce.[37] A heightened imagination and an ability to tap into novelty at that phase carry the risk of succumbing to the irrational—even psychotic—sources of the creative gift.

In sum, when the micro-transition of the mind/brain state settles at, or has a dominant focus, early in the process, one that is proximate to drive and its immediate derivatives, instead of discharging into acts or objects, adjustments in behavior are based on an adaptation of need to perceptual immediacy. Within a category of instinctual drive, novelty accompanies recurrent behavior, but it is also the source of modifications in response to external conditions. There is no elabora-tion of the process underlying novelty, rather, its utilization for innovative solutions to immediate circumstances. When the dominant focus in human mind is at the world surface, novelty takes the form not of subjective experience, but of continuous change in the objects of perception.

Thus, accentuation at early segments relating to instinctual drive gives problem-solving as an adaptive strategy, while a focus on the final outcome captures apparent novelty in the presumed causal change of world objects. When, in the context of a fully unfolded mental state, i.e. object-consciousness, the focus is at intermediate segments of imagery, i.e. when the individual is centered in the whole-part relations of imaginal thought, subject/predicate or topic/attribute relations, ordinarily traversed and given up in the adaptation to

---

[37] Of whom Jung is reputed to have said to Joyce, you're swimming in it, she's drowning.

conscious perception, the sources of creativity are uncovered. An elaboration of the phase occurs merely by withdrawal, as in dream, when the phase is not derived to conscious perception.

Whole-part relations occur at every phase in the mental state, but in imagery the accretion, recruitment, conflation, overlap and decanting of attributes, essentially "mechanisms" of the dream-work,[38] the transition across related attributes (parts) to separate categories (wholes), and the reverse, the evocation by attributes of related categories, or the incorporation in a category of novel properties, all serve to facilitate the growth of thought. The individuation of object- and lexical-semantic concepts within expanded category boundaries accounts for the unity and coherence of the central idea, which, in the partition, trickles into every derivative. In this process, novelty is unchanged, though creativity is an elaboration out of novelty parsed to an adaptive outcome in conscious thought and action.

Consciousness is essential to human creativity, but the growth of ideas is largely unconscious. The plasticity of the unconscious escapes a fixation on reason and conscious objects. Creative ideas that become conscious do not originate in conscious thought. Rational thinking and problem-solving seem confined to consciousness, but the trajectory of every momentary state, in a passage to consciousness, invariably entrains unconscious phases. Moreover, without consciousness there is no distinction of conscious and unconscious; one is awake and aware but not conscious in the human sense, as in animals. It is unlikely that animals, which presumably lack imagery, propagate concepts similar to the human mind, for which a conscious/unconscious divide is fundamental. Consciousness is presumed to be the most highly evolved faculty but unconscious fantasy requires opposition to conscious mind. Given that consciousness is a relation, not an agency, and that a partial suspension of consciousness is necessary for creative thought, the potential for creativity, though abetted by consciousness, may be the principle advance in the evolution of human thought.

---

[38]   See discussion of the von Domaris effect in Brown (2015).

As noted, in most organisms innovative solutions appear in the resolution of drive-based need with adaptation to exigencies in the environment. Every organism, to survive, has to avoid repetition and rote behavior. Invariance and pre-dictability can lessen the chances for survival. Given the imperatives of drive, novelty enables a deviation from non-habitual action, or variation in a behavioral repertoire, though still within the category of a drive-based response. Such behavior may seem creative, but there is no actual elaboration of thought, only the application of whole/part relations, e.g. adjustments of predation according to changing circumstances. Novelty is the defense against inflexibility, while creativity is episodic novelty in the service of concepts. *There is tension between novelty and repetition in instinctual behavior, as between creativity and habit in thought. In creators, habit is generally confined to skill, while creativity applies to concepts for which skill is a means of implementation.* However, even in highly creative people, recurrence of style or theme makes a work recognizable across different products. Schopenhauer wrote that he only had one idea. Bergson and other philosophers have written much the same. It was said of Vivaldi that he wrote not 600 concerti but one concerto 600 times. Aside from copies of the original, a Rembrandt, a Picasso or Rothko is usually easily identified. *One could say that without skill, creativity is helpless, and without creativity, skill is lifeless.*

Creators have an urge to avoid repetition and often stake out new domains for exploration. The shift to neuroscience in Nobelists such as Crick or Edelman, points to a desire for another great work in a different area. However, it is rare that individuals produce a major work in a second field. The impulse to a break with past achievement for another creation or discovery, that is, to be free of past ideas that have become tiresome, facile and predictable, is so strong it can lead to unfortunate outcomes. James Papez did groundbreaking work on the limbic system, but in later years published articles describing micro-organisms in the brains of schizophrenics. Raymond Dart, a scientist I greatly admire, especially for his ingenious papers on the evolution of brain and handedness, finally achieved recognition for the discovery of the Taung skull, but then reported what he thought to be signs of fire use on animal bones in proximity to Australopithecine remains, even naming his discovery A. prometheus, fire-making man. Dart went from ignominy to celebrity to ridicule when the blackish discoloration was later found to be bat guano. The urge to creation and discovery, even after achieving it, can be the basis of later humiliation

6. One or Many Forms of Creativity

Studies of the gifted have been interpreted by some, e.g. Gardner (1983), as indicating multiple forms of intelligence, along with topic-specific memory and other cognitive skills. This argument is clearly an extension of componential or modular theory to the problem of creative thought, for which there is little evidence, apart from descriptions of genius personalities and the incomprehensibility of prodigies like Mozart or Mendelsohn in music, Rimbaud in poetry or Gauss in mathematics.[39] Certainly there is a difference between musical, mathematical and literary genius, and those gifted in one field rarely have talent for another, but this does not mean these abilities are located in, or mediated by, different areas or systems in mind/brain process.

Take the occurrence of early genius in music or mathematics. For those so gifted, the proficiency is like acquiring another language, thus the early appearance and accelerated facility. The individual has musical or mathematical ideas, thinks in the language of music or mathematics and articulates ideas in the grammar of that language. In music, as in the transition to an utterance, a chord, a melody, partitions to constituents that can become subsidiary musical ideas. A theme and variations correspond to a concept and its individuations, or a mathematical idea and its proof.

In music, the theme undergoes a variation that unpacks the idea in a process identical to language production. In most

---

[39]   Gardner begins with a plea for open-mindedness, but goes on to equate intelligence with problem-solving, and declares that he is firmly in the modular camp.

examples of great music, the progression of a work does not occur in a haphazard or additive manner, or by including ancillary melodies, but rather, by an exploration of phrases (sub-categories) within a single motif or musical idea. Musical composition is literary creation in another language, though in literature, meanings are fundamental, while in music they are not apparent except to the composer. The presumption is that music and language employ a common process, not different mechanisms.

As to memory, it makes little sense to posit a "modality-specific store", since memory — more widely, experience — excels in domains of early exposure, deep interest and unwavering commitment. If one considers other fields in which an individual may be considered a genius, such as chess, choreography, architecture or couture, in what sense do special skills represent independent modules or genetically-determined capacities, if the human genome has, as is likely, in spite of suggestions as to recent devolution, remained the same for 50,000 years, ever since the brain ceased to significantly evolve? It is inconceivable that genes for specific talents, such as reading, were present in the Paleolithic brain, pre-dating by thousands of years their appearance as functional abilities. On the basis of observation, pathological effects or experimental study, some have postulated that reading — even font recognition — owes to a specific and genetically-determined module, but the majority of people on earth are illiterate. If the claim is that capacities underlying genius are encapsulated, how could such components appear on a genetic or morphogenetic basis if the modern brain is identical to that of cave-dwellers?[40]

If modes of creativity represent offshoots of normal cognition, the effort should go into identifying process and continuity, not demarcation and spatial arrangement. The prior

---

[40] Capacities in the gifted may be preferentially spared or involved in pathology. I have seen instances in which beautiful orthography, fine surgical technique or rhetorical skill were relatively intact until the late stages of Alzheimer's disease. Conversely, some conditions first involve well-developed skills. An example is the choreographer, George Balanchine, who had ataxia as an unusual presentation of a rare dementia, precisely in the area of his creative work.

discussion of music and language illustrates the rationale for this claim. Systems for action are not output devices; they are hierarchic structures of rhythmic levels that develop over growth planes in the evolution of forebrain. Early rhythms organized about archaic brain systems involve oscillatory mechanisms for postural and axial motility, as in the gait of animals. The rhythm partitions to a higher frequency for running or a slower tempo for stalking. In higher animals, the rhythm for distal and asymmetric movement partitions to the fine frequencies necessary for paw and digital movement.

Music and language are acquired over this structure of kinetic rhythms, oscillatory levels or melodic frequencies, evolving as spandrels of action-systems essential to bodily movement. At some point, the rhythmic motility expands into the musculature for vocalization, from a background rhythm for the speech melody or the intonation pattern. In other words, music and language, probably music first, developed as by-products of action, not as supernumerary functions, but as offshoots in the primary axis of evolutionary growth.

While language has clear adaptive value, this is less obvious for music, though rhythmic noise, hitting a tree, clapping, alarm and distress calls, sounds made with animal horns or a drum, adjustments of beats or change in rate or volume, repetition and delay, provide cues for survival to members in a tribe. Language could evolve out of grunts and calls that signal danger, food or separation. Eventually, a sequence of primitive vocalizations, consonant or consonant-vowel pairs, conveys more complex information and serves as a starting point for the gradual discovery of language. Gesture can precede, supplement or replace language. Pointing is like deictic naming. The combination of gestural language and rhythmic vocalizations with repetitious bodily movements in primitive dance, as in prayer, trance, etc.,[41] provide a construct out of which language and song develop.

With regard to early development of genius and talent, it is well-known that there is a critical period for language learning,

---

[41]   Think of dervishes, davening or Buddhist chants.

after which, without exposure, as in isolated or feral children, language acquisition is limited. Fluency in language acquired after the closure of this window rarely overcomes the speaker's native accent. Giftedness in music and mathematics shows a similar pattern in its relation to language, though fluency in these fields, as in language, can be later acquired. This is the case with skill in technique. The vast majority of violin and piano virtuosi begin study in early childhood. There is variation in ability, just as some children learn motor and verbal skills faster than others, or have better articulation or a wider vocabulary.

The rapid acquisition of language in children has led many linguists to postulate an innate capacity, which implies genetic determination and a dedicated module in the brain. However, variations in timing, in facility, and in the role of maturational factors, except for intelligence, have yet to be worked out. The arguments against evolutionary gradualism are specious, in that they imply a mutation or language gene — for some, even a gene for a particular grammatical rule.[42] This extreme modularity has been transposed to accounts of other exceptional abilities, a presumption that follows from the importance of syntax to language and the difficulty understanding how grammar, including recursive strategies like embedding, could evolve. However, one gets by in a foreign country with a vocabulary of 30–50 nouns and verbs, so it is likely that the decisive step was not the appearance of syntax but the expression of meaning through phonology.[43]

---

[42] This goes with a critique of studies in apes that show a limited degree of language ability. The argument is that labeling is not language, and that a capacity for syntax has not been demonstrated. However, a strong case can be made that naming, or linking a meaning to an object or sign, clearly shown in apes, is an early phase in language acquisition, especially since regions of temporal lobe involved in language are dedicated in monkeys to identifying an object in an array, similar to producing a word out of a lexicon or isolating the word out of the potential for a multiplicity of others.

[43] I have argued for this elsewhere in relation, *inter alia*, to aphasia, that lesions of the primary anterior and posterior language zones give phonological (phonemic, phonetic) deficits.

It is evident that the ability to learn a language is similar to the learning curve of prodigies in other fields, but rapid learning does not imply creative ability. In fact, some creators are slower than normal. One line of inquiry this suggests is that, for creativity, fluency in acquisition, whether rapid or slow, must be accompanied by a prolongation of the juvenile (neoteny), not only in maturation but in the unfolding of the mental state, i.e. delay at a phase of imagery in micro-temporal transition. A delay at early stages, in cognition and in morphogenesis, i.e. in the epigenetic transition from code to structure, is characteristic of evolutionary advance (and aberration). It is not surprising that high and low intelligence are more prominent in male infants at both ends of the spectrum.

The account of brain structure as a residue of process, or of process as four-dimensional structure, implies that recurrent process consolidates patterns of traversal to lay down structure, or that structure is the form assumed by process over a series of recurrences. In evolutionary (morphogenetic) growth, structure is not a stable electrical circuit that emits or outputs function, nor a compilation of genetically-determined dedicated components that implement mental software, but a signature of a dynamic that, over well-traveled paths, establishes subtle biases in configurations that lay down behavior.

In sum, with respect to creativity, this means that genius, even talent, does not depend on autonomous systems, pre-wired circuits or discrete components, but on a wave-front distributed over evolutionary growth planes, the characteristics of which vary among individuals according to the nature of the task, prior exposure, age of acquisition, confidence, dedication, the specificity of experience, selectivity in the traversal, imagery attuned to a particular topic, the ability to retreat to antecedents from surface mind, and the fluidity of whole/part relations in dream and the imagination.

7. Creation Out of What?

Creation is not *ex nihilo*, but entails novel patterns of variable complexity, feeling and refinement, with the totality of personal experience decanted in the work. In some instances, such as a novel, the author draws on a wide range of experience; in other instances, such as a quartet, the range is limited.

In all instances, however, the process is the same, namely, unpacking a concept or category into some form of expression. This might be a very brief musical sequence, as in a composition by Alban Berg, or a quartet or symphony; in vocal music, a song, a cycle of songs, or an aria in an opera. In writing it may be a short story or brief poem, a lengthy essay, novel or poetic work, or an epic of Homeric proportions. In a poem, expression is often compressed, a density that is gradually unraveled in a novel. In poetry, a concentrated immediacy of imagery, feeling and meaning is, in the best poems, conveyed with insight and/or beauty, not only in meaning but in word-sound.

It may well be that when an inspired moment occurs it is independent of the fluency of composition, which depends on putting the inspired idea into some mode of expression. Creativity would seem to refer more to having the idea, or its development, than its composition, but the idea is only apparent when it is fully expressed, while composition is dependent on repeated access to the idea and skill in its rendition. With a brilliant creator and clarity in the idea, composition is rapid and assured. The transition from idea or image to words, notes, etc. is more accessible to study than the gradual development of the idea, which is mostly unconscious. The former, e.g. the passage from concept to word, or a selection from potential, is a parsing of possibility, with choices at every stage as to the most perfect form, e.g. in meaning, phrasal structure, word-choice and sound. The latter is a process of growth as the idea and its virtual constituents take shape, less by partition than propagation within an abstract frame.

If there is symmetry in the growth of an idea and its realization, does what goes into a work differ from what comes out? The development of a concept through an overlap of attributes enlarges the concept from within by whole-part relations. In composition, adding a line or verse, or inserting a passage from another source, may seem adventitious, but in major works the addition is integrated in such a way as to more fully convey the primary theme. The concept searches for modes of expression, at times finding them by accident, but often they arise endogenously. In either case, an addition retraces the same path as a spontaneous ingredient, passing through unconscious process to perception, and in the course of this traversal, issuing from a category that is integrated with the creative idea and then, though appearing to come to the creator from outside, developing from category to item in a manner similar to that of concealed ingredients that arise in the unconscious.

That is, constituents arise spontaneously in the course of composition, as well as from secondary sources, e.g. a citation, a purloined phrase or melody; but in all instances of superior work, the primary category melds diverse ingredients as it strives to expression. The utilization of secondary material does not imply an external relation, since all material—relevant or not, conscious or unconscious—traverses phases in the mental state in the same way. The difference is that perceptions are apprehended as extraneous, while endogenous contents surface in behavior or composition. One might say adventitious material differs from that which is ingredient in that the selection of the latter is unconscious, while the former, having passed through unconscious segments, only seems to enter the work at a conscious endpoint. This implies that regardless of the source of the content, its potential and selection are constitutive, not accidental.

Many creators begin a work uncertain where it is going, except perhaps for a general inclination or direction. A single word or glance can ignite an idea and composition begins at once. Then it seems the work is created instantly or in the process of composition. We tend to think that an unconscious idea is guiding the pen, and I believe this to be the case, but it may well be that composition incites the relevant category to pour out further constituents. This raises a question concerning the speed in which a creative idea is formed. In major works, there is probably a period of gestation or unconscious brewing, but it is conceivable that a creative idea forms quickly, its framework and potential developing all at once. Unconscious ingredients may occur simultaneously, though composition takes place over time. We suspect a gradual ripening, partly because it is difficult to imagine a complex work developing all at once or in a brief interval, and partly because the time taken to compose the piece presumes a comparable sequence in its formation, even though an idea may be apprehended as a whole. There is, however, another way of conceptualizing the creative process that depends on a theory of subjective time experience. The problem is best approached by a consideration of dream-time, in which the spontaneity of creation and an event-sequence compressed in an immediacy on waking provide evidence that the process of thought, and especially creative thought, relates to unconscious time-experience (see below).

In sum, the process of unpacking involves the expansion of wholes and their discharge in composition. Both the formative process and the realization of the concept involve a fractionation of categories; in the one, multiplication of constituents, in the other, partition. One process mirrors the other. Moreover, a fully formed idea is not essential to inspiration or composition, since the products of thought can be on-line with creative effort. Given the similarities of ideation and composition, i.e. generation and expression of an idea, the process guiding the one may concur with that informing the other.

Some ideas are spontaneous, others result from rumination. In the same way, composition can be effortful or immediate. In artists of the first rank, labored work is not inconsistent with genius. Great writers such as Joseph Conrad, though not writing in his native Polish, described the agony that went into every word. However, for most artists the best work is spontaneous, and within a work, the best portions are usually fluent and automatic with little need for revision. Eckermann said of Goethe that genius doesn't struggle to reach the heights, genius soars. Shakespeare and Mozart were famously quick in composition. A handful of great philosophers could dictate a book without correction. In rare individuals, the material is fully available, possibly in consciousness, while in most others, composition is slow, painful and episodic as words (notes, equations) sample and discharge the idea.

8. Creativity and Serial Order

The formation of an idea and its expression should not be conceived in terms of building-blocks and their reassembly. For inspired ideas, or those occurring in a vision or a dream, the constituents are fully integrated, often composed or unpacked "inside-out", with insertions embedded in contexts, not add-ons. Recursion is more pronounced than succession, at least in a struggle to compose. It is fundamental to creative work that intuition, in spite of some accounts of apprehending a work all at once in the mind, is ordinarily not accompanied by a full awareness of all the constituents. The formative process is discovered – or uncovered – in the course of composition.

Intuition is the awareness of a simultaneous construct of variable clarity that is pressing to actualize in serial order. The shift from the idea to its realization gives the impression of a transition from a spatial whole to temporal parts. The whole is conceived as a matrix or schema, vague or clear, from which ingredients are elicited, not necessarily in a specific form or order. The final shape and sequence will be determined by adaptive sculpting and revision. The constituents and the order in which they occur are co-dependent, but not tightly linked, in that the final narrative may require many attempts, e.g. deletion, cut-and-paste, but it seems unlikely that the constituents of an idea are assembled piecemeal in a spatial entity. I would argue that constituents exist – to the extent they do exist – as a hierarchy of virtual phases, with the order of constituents simultaneous until discharge. *The unconscious source, formation and ingredients of an idea, the simultaneity of intuition, and the occurrence of creative ideas in dream, invoke a relation to dream cognition, in which events are "gathered up" prior to actualization on waking.* An example of this phenomenon, and an introduction to the problem and its possible solutions, discussed below, is the dream of Maury described by Freud.

Chapter 8

Introspection and Imagery

*The inner voice or vision is an image
in the mind where it originates*

For an individual mind, the world is universally subjective, but as a local phenomenon, the limits of the subjective are defined by contrast with the objective. The world for the young child becomes a community of objects as an outcome of sensibility that induces a "mitosis" of the subject into inner and outer portions. In the infant, the continuum of the subjective field incorporates the maternal breast or nourishing object. Sensibility ruptures the intra-psychic by objectifying extra-psychic space. The transition is abrupt, as the inner field partitions to subjective and objective portions, the latter so adapted to the physical world that it becomes fully independent and distinct from its psychic antecedents. The fractionation of inner and outer continues. The inner partitions to a self in relation to other mental contents; the outer is filled by a variety of distinct objects.

Gradually, within the subject, the core condenses to a self in relation to other mental contents, i.e. feelings or affect-ideas, and images: visual, verbal, memorial and others. The base of the inner world is an unconscious core anterior to a conscious liminal self in the unidirectional actualization of the mental state. In the core, instinctual drive and the animal inheritance coalesce as categorical primes, including beliefs and values. This construct is delivered into the explicit self, and then, through the self, to imagery and objects. The world is a model of physical reality created by the self or subject to which it feels in opposition. The outer world, i.e. the externalized surface of the mental state, undergoes a parallel fractionation. Sensibility carves out discrete objects, which come to be perceived as independent of the mind in which they originate. Mental contents in consciousness are primarily the verbal images of inner speech or those of the visual imagination. Dynamic imagery is a mode of thought, vivid or subdued, antecedent to objects. Introspection is the term for a self that is conscious of imagery or feeling. An unspoken mental statement or proposition is a verbal image with a high degree of adaptive value. The fact that imagery or conscious thought develops at an intermediate segment in the mind/brain state conforms to the evolutionary principle that new growth occurs at penultimate stages, not endpoints of specialization.

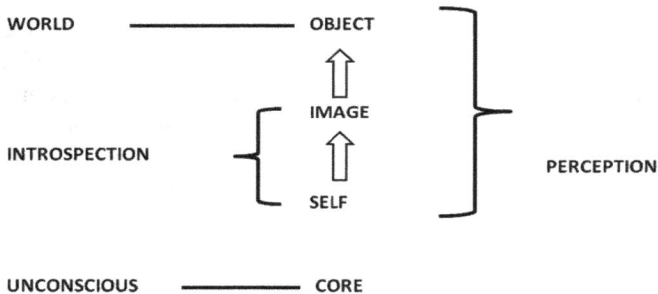

WORLD ——————— OBJECT

IMAGE

INTROSPECTION

SELF

PERCEPTION

UNCONSCIOUS ——————— CORE

Fig. 8.1: All perception and experience is implicit or explicit in the mind/brain state. The transition is from core to conscious self, through which acts, objects and feelings are specified. At some point in development, an intermediate phase of imagery comes to the fore with a relative suspension of objects. When the phase is traversed without evoking an image, the self is in direct relation to objects. This is ordinary perception. When the self is in relation to images in the context of a complete object-development, this is introspection. When the image actualizes as an endpoint, i.e. without sensibility and object-consciousness, the state is dream.

It is essential to understand that the imagery of introspection occurs in the context of a waking state of object-consciousness. Imagery can go in several ways: it can be the focus of reflection or recollection, or the vehicle of imaginative thought; it can actualize as an endpoint in dream or hallucination; or the substrate of the image, not the actual image, can be transformed to an object. The image is an incomplete object; the object is an externalized image, i.e. the substrate of the image is sculpted to an object by sensation. In perception, brain formations that mediate dream are now phases in the forming object, which develops over the same path. This explains why auditory hallucinations replace auditory perceptions, and why one cannot perceive and hallucinate at the same time in the same locus of the visual field. The continuity of waking and dream imagery, their conformance to the "laws" of category/item transition, the propagation or substitution by way of topic/ attribute relations, and the dependence on whether the individual is asleep or awake, help to explain the role of the dream and waking imagination in creative thought.

Moreover, as discussed, in order to access the imagination, it is necessary to withdraw from, but not abandon, the world of objects. If the object world is lost, as in dream, the image, though creative, can undergo distortion. This occurs in sensory deprivation studies, in which subjects lose objects, hallucinate and show alterations of personality. For the creative imagination, the object world must be present, but in the background. This is accomplished by concentration, meditation, darkness, seclusion, even drugs, whatever works. As mentioned, many artists, especially writers, have ways of inducing a mood, which by definition is not oriented to an object, but is inner-directed and receptive to imagery. The goal is for the "inner eye" to predominate, while the outer world is dormant. When the background world is lost or unattended, the imagination, liberated from adaptive pressure, shows creative power that many wish could be experienced in waking consciousness. Creative insight that occurs in dream represents imagery unconstrained by the habit and sensibility the artistic mood seeks to overcome.

In sum, out of the subjectivity of infant mind, a world objectifies. There is progressive fractionation within inner and outer moieties of the subjective. The inner portion begins with a core out of which an explicit self develops. The outer segment divides into an object field that appears mind-independent. The segregation of the mental from the external is the outcome of a process of specification. This process solidifies a boundary that, in the infant, is a continuous transition. Within the subjective portion, along with the specification of the self, an intermediate zone of imagery develops. The relation of the self to objects and images is the basis of consciousness and intentionality.

Images can be deviant in dream, fluid and creative in imagination, or veridical in inner speech and eidetic imagery. Presumably, this depends on the proximity of the image to the intra-psychic surface and the degree to which other modalities of cognition are entrained. When imagery is confined to one modality, e.g. language, as in auditory (speech) hallucination, it is initially perceived as unreal (though this changes if the hallucination is chronic), since a real world actualizes through other unaffected modalities. When more than one modality or component is involved, the image becomes real. A visual hallucination, felt to be illusory, will be perceived as real when it incorporates audition, e.g. a face that speaks. The multi-modality of dream, like that of wakefulness, endows those states with a feeling of realness. The fact that dream imagery affects modalities "across the board", i.e. involves all cognitive domains, leaves no modality to achieve a veridical object that could disconfirm the realness of imagery. This creates a kind of conspiracy of the senses, as in waking perception or multi-modal hallucination which supports the feeling of realness.

In sleep, imagery is without adaptive constraints, engaging mental process diffusely. The diffuseness or generality of dream, and the lack of constraints in a truncated mental state, allow personal experience, meaning-relations, symbolism and feeling to dominate the image-formation. In addition, the self is passive, agency is diminished and space is foreshortened; viscous with an instability in which one image melts into another. These phenomena contribute to the otherworldliness of the dream. In wakefulness, the phase of imagery is given over to object-formation. Focal pathology exposes the category/item relations that govern this process when the effect is restricted to one cognitive domain, e.g. language, visual perception. The same process is involved in dream substitution and pathological symptom-formation, but the symptoms of focal lesion are more specific, less related to belief, feeling and personal experience.

In introspection, withdrawal allows ancestral phases in the object to come to the fore. The imagery of conscious reflection is more veridical than in dream since the individual is conscious, with habit and sensory constraints impacting the formative process. Consciousness of objects, though in abeyance, continues during creative thought, sustaining the effects of sensibility on pre-perceptual content. This provides boundaries on image-formation, so it does not drift off and become irrelevant to the problem at hand.

1. Dream and Waking Consciousness

In psychoanalysis, the presumed function of dream is to preserve sleep, a slim justification for so important a phenomenon. On the microgenetic view, dream imagery is an inevitable consequence of the capacity for introspection, since imagery is an obligatory segment in human perception, consciousness and intentionality. Animals perceive objects without demonstrable imagery, but given the lack of a self-concept, waking imagery is unlikely, in spite of anecdotes or neurophysiological studies showing cell discharge in sleep similar to that on a waking task. If so, visual imagery in dream is also unlikely, since dream is an accentuation of the imagination in the absence of conscious perception. In humans, waking and dream images have a spectator. An objectless or imageless state of consciousness is just a theoretical possibility. The subject/object distinction in animals accounts for the perception of objects, but without a self, and absent a subject/object divide, who or what is looking at the dream image?

It may be there is a state of "sciousness" (James, 1899; Bricklin, 2015) prior to a subject/object relation (which is often the aim of meditation and the goal of other regressive techniques, e.g. hypnotic trance, mystical descent), but the state would have to be preliminary to the partition of the subjective world. I am skeptical that a generalized state of subjectivity, without a subject or an object, exists apart from a vegetative awareness. This is consistent with the idea that a subject cannot exist without an object, and the reverse, the absence of a dream image is coma-like sleep. Moreover, the dream image requires a distinction between self and mental content. Animals lacking subject-centeredness, a core self or self-concept, without a distinction of conscious and unconscious, but with a subject/object distinction, would not be conscious in a remotely human sense. If sciousness is a precursor to con-sciousness, one should find it in animals close to humans on the evolutionary scale. Perhaps sciousness is fetal consciousness. In any event, REM in animals does not signal dream, since human research shows a weak correlation.

The present account makes several assumptions that run contrary to general opinion. First, the idea that dream and imagination are separate phenomena is disputed. Instead, the claim is that imagination is a benign form of dream, or dream restrained by sensibility, closer to the external situation. Second, the argument that animals have dream activation without psychic accompaniment contradicts opinions based on observations of pets and inferences from some experimental studies. However, the finding that REM activity goes back to primitive mammals, perhaps as far as marsupials, suggests that whatever the function of dream may be, e.g. memory reinforcement, it requires the reactivation of neural circuits, not the presence of imagery. Finally, though I find the sequence from imagination to dream imagery persuasive, there may be objection to the position that, in evolution, the conscious phenomena of imagery precede those of dream given that dream is presumably the more primitive phenomenon.

In a word, the evolution of self in relation to imagery makes dream-imagery possible, though animals may be in a dream state without imagery. The problem is that the word "dream" implies a state of imagery during sleep, while the presumed correlation with REM and EEG activity provides a physical marker for a dream state. The finding in humans that dream imagery and REM dissociate, i.e. dream without REM and REM without dream, means that the physical markers identify a state of activation but not necessarily one of dream-imagery. This means that the imagery of dream is not essential to the physiological dream state, which could occur in animals without imagery.

Freud and others have argued that dreaming usually revives the least-noticed fragment of day-time perception, unlike animal studies that purport to show the recurrence of neural discharge associated with an over-learned task. Further, there are reasons for dream imagery, e.g. resolution of conflict, "wish fulfillment", but what purpose is served by dream imagery in animals? Certainly, it would not serve to maintain sleep, firstly, because sleep is a state of vulnerability in animals, and secondly, because the imagery could have no psychological function comparable to that postulated in man. More likely, activation of the brain in sleep serves some physiological purpose independent of imagery. This could be a general effect, such as facilitation of networks, the recruitment of neurons or reinforcement of behaviors, or it could be a specific effect, such as periodic heightening of arousal or preparatory reactions, or "consolidation" of memory and learning. In human mind, the return to imagination is a flight from objectivity, but a revival of the objective is the natural destination of mind and creative thought.

If, as argued, the relative suspension of object-formation with a dominant focus on imagery is the basis of inward or reflective thought, it is also the basis of intentionality, in the relation of the self to a desired, imagined or hypothetical object. Waking imagery tends to be more focused, closer to rational thought and the external situation. The relation of self to image is preserved in dream, though the dream self is more passive and the imagery more fluid and distorted than in waking. The dream image is what happens to waking imagination in the abeyance of external sensation and internal habit. Presumably, the imagery of dream involves similar neural formations to that of wakefulness. One could say that waking imagery, which arises at pre-object phases in microgeny, exploits the physiological bases of non-imaginal dream in animals as a substrate for the waking imagination. On this view, dream is an inevitable consequence in sleep when constraints on object-formation are lifted. Dream images are a byproduct of waking mental imagery and the capacity for creative imagination, essential to human thought and representing a singular advance in the evolution and maturation of the human mind.

Chapter 9

Time, Dream and Creativity

The creative awakens to the world out of the dream-time

The celebrated dream of Maury consists of a lengthy series of events in revolutionary France, leading to capture, trial, imprisonment and death by guillotine. The dreamer's head was in the block and as the knife fell he was awakened by the headboard falling on his neck. Freud could not believe the dream-events were invented instantaneously, and presumed the narrative was pre-packaged and triggered on waking, but this is too facile an explanation for a dream that, as with others, poses deep and complex problems on the nature of subjective time. For one thing, Freud's explanation does not account for the concurrence of the knife and the headboard at that precise moment, with a reinstatement of antecedent events, coherent with and leading to the final one that terminates the dream. While the dream is unusual in its duration and detail, it is common for environmental stimuli to be incorporated in dream. In one of my dreams, I awoke hearing church bells instead of the ring of an alarm clock, a common substitution. While the preceding events all seemed to lead to the assimilated bells, how is the occurrence of an alarm, or headboard, transformed to the related dream content and how does the final event occur in the context of an appropriate sequence of antecedent events?

As to the transformation of the headboard or alarm to the dream content, the phenomena of dream are linked to objects by bridging properties. For example, a penis becomes the image of a knife in dream because of the overlap of the attributes of shape and penetration. Similarly, the headboard resembles a blade in its trajectory, in its potential for severing the neck and sudden fall. There is also the "head" in the guillotine and "headboard."[44] The alarm resembles church bells that signal an awakening, or an arousal to work or to prayer. The mentality of dream consists in combining disparate objects with shared properties. Regarding temporal order, that is a more complicated story.

Freud, and before him von Hartmann (1893), believed the unconscious was timeless, but timeless phenomena do not exist, so it is preferable to say that events in the unconscious are simultaneous: that is, dream-events, or experiential contents that remain beneath consciousness (regardless of whether or when they occur in life, or their sequence in unconscious thought), appear in dream cognition in a stratification that is temporally-ordered but not necessarily in the original form or order of occurrence in life, or even in the dream. A waking experience transformed in dream may have occurred in the distant or recent past, but all events occur in the present of the dream (Fig. 9.1).

Creative thought resembles dream in many respects: (1) the major role of the unconscious; (2) the occurrence of metaphor, connotation and similar characteristics of primitive (animistic) thought, e.g. the von Domarus effect (1944);[45] (3) accounts of creativity in dream; (4) recall of the totality of a dream on waking, and the whole of a creative work on inspiration; and (5) the influence in both of early events on mature cognition. The effects of childhood experience on adult thought and behavior are obvious, but in artistic creativity they can be profound. So many themes in literary works derive from, or are reinforced by, events early in life. Indeed, the influence of such events is almost essential in creative artworks. The relation to early experience and memory in dreams and creativity is part

---

[44] The French term, dosseret, refers to a backboard, is not as explicit as in English, though still located at the head of the bed, tête de lit.

[45] In Aboriginal culture, the dreamtime is the source of the creative spirit.

of the subjectivity of art. Thus, while a journalist writes of current events, the novelist or poet draws on early and personal experience. A similar distinction holds for the photographer or documentary film maker and painters or creative directors.

Art differs from science in this respect, that the closer to objectivity, to fact and present experience, the less the imaginative content, and, ordinarily, the less creative the outcome. This can be explained by the concurrence of the distant and recent past in unconscious cognition, and the resultant influence of personality formation and childhood experience on adult mentation. The temporal distance from child to adult is erased in the simultaneity of the unconscious. The spatial whole accessed briefly in intuition points to the simultaneity of cumulative events in the dream image, as the whole of a dream is apprehended momentarily on waking before it fades in the shadows.

The unconscious simultaneity that accounts for the mixture of recent and childhood events in both dream and creative thought is consistent with psychoanalytic teachings, if not the conflicts and mechanisms of orthodox theory. If events are simultaneous, for example if the events in Maury's dream, though ordered, are "represented" simultaneously, they will be selected, on waking, in an order that is likely to be faithful to that in dream, but more importantly, the order must make sense to the dreamer. Thus, if Maury was awakened by the sound of water, the dream might well have ended with drowning in his prison cell or with rain in the courtyard leading to the guillotine. The imagery incorporates the precipitating stimulus, but actualizes regardless of what that stimulus is, since an external occurrence that awakens a dreamer, once assimilated in the fabric of the dream, has many possibilities to effect the progression of events.

Moreover, a dream has greater meaning than a comparable sequence in wakefulness, with the search for meaning continuing after the dream expires. This occurs in art, but not ordinarily in life. Usually, meaning is spread over all events in dream, as in an artwork, such that any one event, unlike waking experience, has no greater import than another. The presence of meaningfulness in dream, or the sense that a dream has a meaning, though not a meaning specific to a particular item or event, may represent the compression of word- or event-meaning in a simultaneity of events. Conscious temporal order heightens the meaning or signification given to dream, and to isolated events within the dream, in a manner comparable to that of an artwork. Meaning in a creative work, in its ideational mode, is not usually assigned to constituents. As in dream, meaningfulness applies to the work as a whole, such as the meaning of a poem or painting.

In sum, events early in a dream co-occur with later ones. There is a tenuous preservation of order in the succession of earlier and later in the dream. The mix of distant and recent memories, or their relation to life-events, is not "tagged" to a veridical sequence. While some dreams have a coherent progression, others are an assortment of seemingly random images. The waking narrative tends to apply a temporal order that is most plausible to the dreamer. Without a past or future, the dream has a knife-edge present, in which the self is a victim or passive spectator without reflection, recall or agency. Dream events may be "stacked" in the order of their occurrence but the shift from simultaneity to temporal order occurs when events actualize in consciousness. A dream is like a memory in waking thought. Events in the dream are perceived in a present that, unlike the duration of the "specious" present, is instantaneous. The time of dream continuously passes, like that in the natural (mind-independent) world. The dream is non-perspectival. Early events are not memories to later ones, since there is no past in relation to the dreamer.

Unlike waking thought, in which events are constantly replaced to become memories, and recognized as past in relation to the present, in the dream, simultaneity and the absence of a past, briefly recognized on waking, assure that all events, to the extent they are recollected, have the potential to participate in the whole of the dream-content. If a dream occupies 10–20 minutes of clock time, all events within the dream are, on waking, transiently available before they are forgotten,[46] and all events occur at the same moment regardless of their position in the duration. The events collapse to an

---

[46]   The similarity to studies in iconic memory is relevant.

immediacy that is recollected on waking. This description also applies to insight in creative thought, in which the whole of a work or theory is glimpsed momentarily. The difficulty in fully recalling a dream, due to the rapid fading of content, corresponds with the effort in composition to tease out and serially depict the intuited but vague content in a creative work.

The distinction of memory and perception is relevant to dream recall and the elicitation of unconscious content in creativity, in that it allows us to identify events as dreams, memories, fantasies or real objects, though at times there is uncertainty as to whether an event is a dream or remembrance. This depends in part on the separation of inner mind and outer world. The feeling of pastness accompanies waking memories, while a transient present accompanies dream. The pastness accentuates interioricity. The presentness of dream owes to its perceptual quality, giving a feeling of realness that, on waking, becomes memory — if the dream is not forgotten. To bring a dream or creative idea from unconscious thought and sub-jectivity into conscious thought and composition, or from the plasticity of imagination to a fixation on perception, entails a transfer of content from the privacy of memory and imagina-tion to the publicity of discourse and communication, as well as from potential to actual or from possibility to commitment. As we know more words than we use or recognize more objects than we encounter, the inability to extract every detail from the dream corresponds to the struggle to evoke words or notes from a creative idea. This agrees with the near-inexhaustibility of ideas of depth and power. An artist or scientist, if fortunate, may have only one idea in a lifetime, but even a long and productive life may be insufficient to fully explore it.

The creative process involves the conveyance of an inner unconscious phase of personal memory to an audience of others. This is also a kind of translation from the language of the unconscious to that of conscious thought and perception. The work must be comprehensible. If not, like the dream it was, it will die with its creation. In science and in art, the translation should commingle with the interests and capacities of others; that is, creativity is midway between fantasy and conversation. The temporal order in composition need not correspond to that in the idea, but there must be a rationale to the sequence, if not for others, then for the creator. This is true even in a painting or sculpture which, though ordered in composition, is not perceived in the sequence of its creation. In science or mathematics, the creative idea, though intuitively apprehended, will have to retrace a series of logical steps, even if those steps did not occur in the discovery, to persuade others of a truth that is self-evident to the creator.

In both creativity and dream, there is a cumulative wholeness of images, some real, some imagined, some transformed. As in dream, the brief presentation of a creative whole is more often the gist of an idea than its content, which may yet have to be distilled. The presentation then distributes into a (literary, musical) narrative that is ordered according to the "laws" of form and harmony and the interpretive skill of the creator. The temporal order of events in a creative work — what is omitted, altered or included — corresponds with what is saved, forgotten or rejected in the narrative of the dream. The psychoanalyst is like a connoisseur of art, more intrigued by what is or is not selected and its meaning to the individual, rather than the precision and order of contents.

As we know, the brief apprehension of the dream as a whole fades rapidly in the effort to maintain it in consciousness or to recall its contents. Since events in the dream may not be precisely ordered until they actualize, or the order may be confounded by seemingly unrelated images, with confusion as to the exactness of event-position, and since the succession in dream is imaginative, and often irrational, not logical, it is unclear to what extent waking recall of the dream sorts out events so as to form a meaningful narrative, or how much the narrative depends on a brief awareness of the succession. Probably, it is a little of both. Accounts of creativity in dream raise similar problems, though many creative ideas, such as Wagner's *Prelude* or Coleridge's *Kubla Khan*, suggest that succession in dream can be preserved. In the case of Wagner, the iterative pattern of the music no doubt aided in its recall, while with Coleridge what is of interest is the recall of the initial verses, not the later ones closer to arousal. This is in accord with the simultaneity of content, in that later dream events (in contrast to the recency effect in memory testing) are not necessarily revived more readily than those of an earlier position.

It is not surprising that the sequence of events in dream, though not conforming to the past/present/future of waking consciousness, does conform to the derivation of phases in the mind/brain state, which is a before/after series. *That is, the series of phases in a single mental state corresponds to the series of states that constitute the content of the dream. More precisely, the phase-transition that lays down a mind/brain state is a non-temporal succession, ordered in a series of before/after phases in a simultaneous epoch until the state actualizes. In a word, simultaneity applies to phases in the mental state, as well as state-succession within the dream.*

The non-temporality of the mind/brain state is identical to that of a succession of states. This gives a parsimonious account of diverse phenomena, i.e. the epochal nature of a mental state, dream and creative thought. It also implies that simultaneity, not timelessness, is the nature of unconscious process, as temporal sequence is the nature of conscious process, and that simultaneity is applicable to all unconscious events, whether the generation of a mental state or a succession of states in dream or creative thought. The postulation of simultaneity may resolve Whitehead's claim of paradoxical non-temporal succession in concrescence with the epochal nature of moment-ary states.

Put differently, the bottom-up succession of phases in the mind/brain state is replicated in the before/after stratification of a series of states in the unconscious. The phase-transition depositing the mind/brain state is inferred from pathology. Successive episodes in dream can be described on waking, while creative ideas are discovered on inspiration or in compo-sition. *This means that the simultaneity of a before/after succession is the mode of unconscious time-experience, for thought and perception, for mental states and mental events, with consciousness of state-succession occurring on awakening, and consciousness of the contents of a creative idea occurring on inspiration and/or composition.*

1. Dream and the Unconscious

Though some philosophers are skeptical, creative and ordinary individuals would affirm the significance of unconscious thought in the germination of ideas and their continuing implementation. Skepticism can be attributed to the obvious fact that, notwithstanding dream, which in any case depends on conscious report and is considered a mode of consciousness, there is no evidence of non-conscious thought outside a state of waking consciousness, and no expectation of cognition other than animal mind. Similarly, studies that access the unconscious, such as masking or priming, are carried out in conscious subjects, so the presence of consciousness is essential for the demonstration of unconscious process. Apart from fictional zombies, sleepwalking, hypnosis or some yet-to-be-described brain pathology, exactly what is referred to in discussing conscious and unconscious as distinct states or processes? The fact is, every waking state is accompanied by consciousness. There is no known state of adult wakefulness, apart from vigilance or the possibility of sciousness, that could be termed non-conscious, no form of brain damage that destroys consciousness leaving the individual awake with other functions intact, and no brain area that mediates consciousness apart from archaic structures, e.g. midbrain, thalamus, which support arousal and the sleep-wake cycle.

Consciousness persists with a loss of objects, as in cortical blindness. When this is combined with cortical deafness, the loss of visual and auditory objects leads to behavior that is psychotic but conscious. To eliminate consciousness, the person would have to be in coma, though perhaps in severe dementia most of the properties that define human consciousness are lost. The enfeeblement is so severe that it is difficult to know what abilities are preserved. If consciousness cannot be peeled off, leaving animal cognition or an automaton, then for the human mind, to be awake is to be conscious, though there are grades of consciousness from lucidity to somnolence, from outer-directed attentiveness to inner-directed concentration (see below).

Consciousness cannot be destroyed without drugs or substantial brain damage, because it is not a thing or function but a relation. In animals and young children, this relation is between the subject as a nidus in subjectivity and the external world. This can be construed as an interface of subjectivity with its objectified portion. The relation is between the pure subjective—a subject, not yet a self—and its outer segment. Subjectivity partitions to extra-personal objects and intra-personal images. Through sensibility, objects detach in a world that is a continuation of the subjectivity of the mental state. Essentially, an earlier phase in the mind/brain state apprehends a later phase in the same state. The self that perceives an object is conscious of its own images, whether intra-psychic or parsed to objectivity by sensibility. The subject/object relation in an infant or young child can be termed awareness.[47] A state of awareness exhibits thought, feeling and adaptive strategies in behavior, but is bereft of an inner life of thought or imagination. Consciousness entails a further partition within the relation of subject to object, namely, a self that perceives objects and is also conscious of pre-perceptual imagery.

Consciousness evolves each moment out of unconscious thought, but the unconscious in a state of consciousness is not the unconscious of dream, in which unconscious process occurs without sensory adaptation. Since dream images actualize when the constraints of consciousness are lifted, it is unlikely that the imagery of dream swirls about beneath a conscious surface, though some "operations" of the dream-work no doubt apply to the cognitive unconscious. Studies of focal lesions uncover unconscious process, and document the whole/part shifts that deliver conscious content. Pathology exposes the process through which potential is transformed. A disruption of unconscious process with focal lesions does not lead to symbolic distortions or bizarre contents, but derailments within an object or lexical category.

The fact that the contents of a recollected dream can, to the dreamer, approximate everyday experience, or can be strange

---

[47]   We may approximate this state when we are not concentrating on some activity, that is, absent-minded, as in driving some distance or avoiding an object in the street, as a sudden realization that, perhaps lost in thought, or not thinking, we have not been conscious of what we were doing.

and incomprehensible, probably represents the degree to which habitual thinking and constraints are imposed on the sequence. The substitutions deciphered by psychoanalysis represent the influence of experiential memory, feeling and meaning-relations on developing images. For example, in dream, a knife may substitute for a penis, but the aphasic will say "spoon" for "knife." The difference represents the reduced impact of personal memory and conceptual-feeling in the aphasic, where the process that is exposed by the lesion is limited to word-finding. In contrast, dream is a generalized regression that displays a mode of syncretic thought from which the aphasic, by virtue of the locality of damage, is spared. The dream illustrates how these phenomena, combined with unfiltered imagery, distort the normal process. The conscious state does not have embedded within it the referents of the dream. The symbolic distortions of dream do not actualize in consciousness because the substrate of the distortion is transformed to an object.

In this connection, there are cases of brain damage or disease in which an unknown artistic performance is "released." For example, persons with brain injury may start to play the piano, draw or paint, which they had never done before. These are not creative performances, but evidence of latent skills that appear to be new occurrences. Generally this is attributed to disinhibition, which presumes a potential for the ability that pre-existed the damage. Though most artists are severely incapacitated by brain damage, especially in writing, there are exceptional cases in which creativity is preserved, perhaps increased. I have written of the case described by Zaimov et al. (1969), a famous Bulgarian artist with a large left hemisphere stroke and total aphasia, whose style shifted from a static social realism to dream-like paintings with thick colors and altered perspective that have been judged by experts as superior to the pre-stroke canvases. Here one has a creative artist who managed to continue with a dramatic change in style. The shift from a literal to a more figurative and dreamy painting may owe to the severe impairment of language and the ascendance of other modes of cognition previously in check.[48]

2. Order and Simultaneity in Dream

Within the dream, earlier events vanish, leaving only awareness for ongoing content. In the "present" of a dream, the dreamer is not aware of antecedents. Only on awakening, with the perception of earlier and later, do prior events come into awareness and the sequence takes on significance. The lack of awareness for prior events while dreaming is consistent with a present that is like the crest of a wave, with a self that arises in the shift from before to after. Less likely, the transition from before to after generates as a memory or partial realization by the waking self of a dream-self that is swept along on the edge of change.

The past in a dream, though lost to the dreamer, is apprehended on waking if the dream as a whole is recalled. The lack of the past to a dreamer does not mean the past is lost. The question is why the dreamer loses the past in the dream, but recalls it on waking. I would propose that the events which constitute the lost past to the dreamer are revived and ordered out of a simultaneous ranking (Fig. 9.1). It is not the simultaneity that accounts for the lost past, since the whole dream is present on waking. Instead, the transition from the whole of a dream (or creative idea) to the temporal order of narration (or composition) is a shift from one mode of time experience to another (the A and B series of McTaggart, 1934/68).

Consciousness of succession in the dream-state does not correspond to consciousness of formative stages in creative ideation. Partly this is due to the implicit, subjective and/or quasi-intentional aim of creative thought, such that an idea or solution to a problem, though not yet known, is the shapeless entity that forms the object of the intention, with the goal as valuable as the formative steps in its realization. These steps are

---

[48]   I have seen the pre- and post-stroke paintings at the National Museum in Sofia and can attest to the shift to a grimmer, darker and more dream-like content. I have also noted similar changes in the paintings of other artists afflicted with brain disorders.

probably not aligned in a sequential manner appropriate to the insight; they may well be a melange of contents, but they can be recovered with careful analysis. Dream also has a subjective aim or at least a progression, story-like, from an incidental or personal context to an outcome that relates to major life decisions. Earlier events tend to proceed to closure as the narrative changes in the course of the development. The events are stacked in the instantaneity of passage. In contrast, the ingredients of creative thought may go back many years, are often complex and difficult to untangle in the duration of a conscious state. That is, on waking, the whole of the dream is briefly present, but the whole of a creative idea may be too extensive to be perceived. This is why composition over time is the equivalent of immediate dream report.

An unforgotten dream recurs in memory when events in their entirety have an actual present to which the succession can relate. On waking, the dream is briefly in the present, but over time its content, if not forgotten, is relegated to the past. Wakefulness creates a present in relation to which the dream-content, like a memory, becomes a past experience. Dream is largely memory content that, like hallucination, is raised to the level of perception. Events in dream are felt as real and perceptual. The difference is that memory is a recollection of past experience, while dream is a reworking that develops on memory content. Thus, perception is productive memory, revived to a veridical object by sensory sculpting. Memory is the revival in waking consciousness of prior experience. Dream is a revival of memory that can be more or less deviant, but without the effects of sensibility. Unlike the memory of a perception, and in spite of the perceptual quality of dream, to remember a dream is to have a memory of a memory, even if the memory undergoes distortion.

State-specificity in recall is likely, and may explain why most dreams are not remembered. The abbreviated perception that is the memorial content of dream, when revived, does not achieve a level to which there is conscious "access", i.e. relaxation of focus or incompleteness in derivation. This occurs because the dream content slips beneath the floor of the present. Since waking perceptions fade to memories, and memories in dream intensify to perceptions, the memorial is more fully evident in dream than in perception, where it is obscured by sensory adaption. In perception, memory is transitional to an object; in dream, memory is the object distorted by lack of adaptive sculpting.

On waking, we realize that a dream was like a real perception, such that the consciousness of dream content is a consciousness of an immediately prior perception. This phenomenon is like an eidetic image, the brief pictorial recall of a perception — at times exceptional in prodigies — that fades to a memory image. Thus, while memories are equivalent to *revived* perceptions, dreams *are* attenuated perceptions with a different pattern of revival. For one thing, waking perception is veridical, unlike dreams that only appear to be so. On revival to memory, perceptions show varying degrees of completion, while dreams — incomplete objects lacking sensory adaptation — display features of primitive mentality, such as symbolism, displacement and condensation, that are ordinarily submerged in waking thought. *Put differently, the incomplete recall of a perception masks layers of hallucination, imagination and dream-like thought that are concealed within the incompleteness, layers that to a variable extent are displayed in dream cognition. These layers are also the source of the creative imagination.*

The quality of unconscious time — events simultaneous in a more or less instantaneous duration — explains the ability to hear a melody, retain and follow a text or film, even though the immediate precedents — words, tones, images — no longer exist in present consciousness. How, in fact, can a no-longer-existing sound be retained in consciousness as a melody subsequent to its perishing? Short-term memory is interpreted as the persistence or ability to "hold onto" recent events, but this does not explain their availability or "continuance" into the present. What does "holding onto" or persistence mean, other than iterated revival? Interpretations of this problem tend to expand the duration of the present to accommodate recent experience or expand (so-called working) memory to accommodate a greater range of activity in consciousness. However, these terminological ploys merely finesse the problem, which is the illusory duration that hovers over the instantaneity of physical passage. Microgenetic theory addresses this problem head-on, postulating that past states are revived in the current state, though increasingly attenuated in each revival. Decay or forgetting is incomplete revival. This applies to immediate dream awareness, in which there is uniform apprehension of early and late contents, though a dramatic event, such as the decapitation in Maury's dream, were it implausibly positioned earlier in the sequence, would be better recalled — if only for its catastrophic effect — than prior or subsequent dream-events.

The revival of the past-in-the-present in waking life is not only for a specific event, but also for the history of the individual, values, beliefs, habits and presuppositions, along with feeling and meaning-relations. The event-to-be-recalled is a superficial plane in this process. It seems likely that the dream-content, though arising out of this personal context, when apperceived in immediate recall, is detached from its diachronic history. The event is an object free of present context, creating an opening for psychoanalytic interpretations. In waking life, for example, when a melody is perceived, the prior tones are revived as part of the experiential history of the individual, which accounts for the feeling, meaning and familiarity of the music. The tones that give continuity to music peel off sequentially in recurrent mental states (Fig. 9.1).

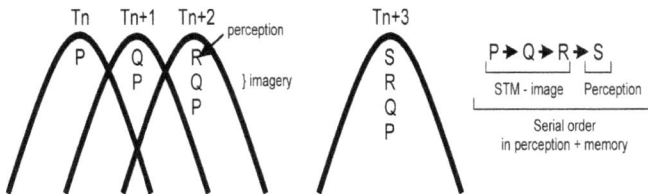

Fig. 9.1: The perception (P) at Tn is replaced at Tn+1 by another perception (Q), which may resemble or differ from that at Tn. Perceptual stability depends on resemblance; change depends on difference. Within the perception at Tn+2 (arrow, R), the mind/brain state revives Tn+1 almost completely, such that the image of P at Tn+2 is prior to the object (Q), and so on. Over a brief succession of mental states, P, Q and R represent images of past perceptions revived to a decreasing extent in the oncoming present, and graded according to this revival. An eidetic image is

a near-complete revival. A memory image is a vague recurrence at some psychic distance from a present object. At Tn+3, the series of images, P, Q and R, forms an order antecedent to the perception (S). The perception and memory of serial order depend on a theory of perception as developing out of memory. Serial order occurs within the present, but depends on succession for the layering of prior experience.

Ordinarily, when an external stimulus becomes part of a dream, the dreamer wakes up. The stimulus is assimilated as a terminal event, not usually in earlier parts of the dream, though if it were we would probably not know it. This gives the impression that the dream was retro-fitted to reconcile the stimulus. In some respects this resembles a creative insight, when sudden enlightenment seems to re-order the unconscious idea to lead inevitably to the conclusion. One might suppose that the contents of the idea, though prioritized, are in no particular order, especially given the long preparation for scientific or mathematical discovery. Presumably, irrelevant data are eliminated, so that what remains assumes an order that justifies the insight.

In this respect, the selection and re-ordering of a scientific idea is a clue to what occurs in dream recall, in which primarily those events that conform to the conclusion are recalled, while unrelated events drop out. If the creative idea is unlikely to be ordered in a logical sequence awaiting final insight, the insight must find order in the contents, some of which are pertinent, others not. In science or mathematics, this process takes place over a long period of study and conceptual growth, yet it corresponds, in the relation to dream, to what is an ordinary nightly occurrence. In both dream and the creative imagination, the event-sequence is infiltrated by unrelated or inappropriate images, which tend to be sorted out on inspiration (composition) and waking. In light of the similarities of dream and dream-recall to creative thought and inspiration, it is not without reason that enlightenment is also referred to as an awakening.

To sum up, there is a correspondence between dream, as a model of unconscious cognition, and creative thought, as exhibiting features in common with dream. There are also commonalties between dream,

*creative thought and myth, in that the past, though very much alive in
the content, ceases to be past for the dreamer or thinker. The unconscious character of these states, when confounded with present experience, carries personal and ancestral memories and the creative
imagination to a vivacity greater than in everyday life.*

As in psychoanalysis, the account of dream as wish-fulfill-
ment, or as a guardian of sleep, or for the working out and
resolution of conflict, as well as the interpretation of dream
imagery, depends on a homuncular theory of content and
mechanism. Psychoanalysis offers a methodology, an analytic
schema and an emphasis on childhood experience similar to
myth, and, one could add, creative thought, especially in the
narrative of interpretation, where events widely separated in
space and time concur in the overlap of attributes and relations
of meaning. Unlike literary works, which require a coherent
narrative for the comprehension of a reader, but similar to
psychoanalysis, myth enjoys a simultaneity of content over
time and space and an eradication of the actual past in favor of
symbolic or paralogical substitutions. As psychoanalysis
attempts to explain personal behavior and the workings of the
human mind, myth provides an account of transpersonal
events and an explanation for physical phenomena in lieu of
scientific theory. Yet by virtue of its success in populating the
psyche with hypothetical agencies, psychoanalysis has done
much to hinder a realistic psychology of the unconscious, to
which, it is hoped, this discussion will contribute.

*Among the similarities of creative ideation and dream are: (1) an
unconscious accumulation of concepts or events that constitute the
dream and comprise the creative idea; (2) the global (epochal) apprehension or simultaneity of the content of dream as perceived on
waking and the creative idea as apprehended in inspiration, (3) the
epochal nature of the mind/brain state that corresponds to the simultaneity of dream and creative ideation; (4) the affinities of waking from a
dream to the wholeness of inspiration in creative insight; (5) the
process of achieving a relatively coherent narrative of often disparate
contents in both dream and creative thought; (6) the concurrence of
earlier- and later-acquired experience, or distant and recent events in
dream and the formative process in creative ideation; (7) the transformation of the memorial to the perceptual, and the reverse; (8) the
many reports of a creative vision in dream; (9) the actualization of*

subjectivity in dream narration, insight and composition; and (10) the
transition from non-temporal succession in a present without dura-
tion to temporal-order in relation to a perspective.

3. Time and Motility

The transition from unconscious simultaneity to conscious time-order appears abrupt, giving the impression of a barrier between two separate worlds, one subjective, one objective, one psychic in relation to brain physiology, the other physical and mind-independent. This transition, which occurs immediately on waking with consciousness of temporal order, or suddenly on insight, is ordinarily mediated by the body. Indeed, paralysis in the dream state gives way to motility on waking as an illustration of the role of action in conscious time-order. The action need not be explicit. The global recall of the dream fades rapidly with speech, ocular or other voluntary movements. Inner or sub-vocal speech, especially focal attention directed at the dream-contents, increases forgetting.[49] Conceivably, the arousal of will or agency entails a shift from the passive dream-self to the active waking-self and carries mentation to a conscious state. The role of the body is most apparent in composition. In working out a creative idea, an artist will type, draw, write or paint by hand, such that the idea seems to flow out of the fingers. Writers frequently mention the mysterious process through which ideas emerge on paper through a pen, their fingers being an extension of their mind, so much so they often feel unable to write without special paper, pen or ink.[50]

This implies that bodily action, including vocalization, even will or agency, is engaged in the transition to external time-order, midway between interior mind and external motion.[51]

---

[49]   As noted, looking at hallucination, even the effort to remain passive in a transitional state leads to disappearance of the image.

[50]   The Eureka effect and eccentricities of artistic thought, along with experiments on problem-solving and fMRI correlation, are discussed in some recent books, e.g. Kounios and Beeman (2015); Irvine (2015), but without an attempt to describe the unconscious process of insight or creativity.

[51]   Guyau (in Michon et al., 1988) noted that a child's reach for an object is the seed of causality and the idea of the future.

An incipient idea, though apprehended briefly in conscious thought, passes to the world through the body. In some instances, such as playing the piano, the transition from a musical idea, score or theme is rapid, in other instances it is slow and labored, but in each case, unlike an object that detaches in the world, the limb is felt as belonging to the body. The body is like an image that does not fully externalize but except for, *inter alia*, vocalization, sign, dance or mime, it acts through other objects. In writing or drawing, the limb is intermediate between composition and idea. In playing an instrument, notes externalize in tones, as limb and finger movements implement the idea through instrumentation. That is, all action is implemented through the body, which, unlike a perception, does not fully externalize. The body is partly in the mind, partly in the world, which may explain the ease of transition to action from other forms of imagery.

The transition to temporality in action can be understood in terms of the shift from unconscious to conscious time. As discussed, an action can be conceptualized as a series of rhythmic levels, beginning with slow rhythms for axial and postural motion and individuating to faster ones for the digital and vocal innervation. The faster rhythms issue from the slower ones, and develop by unpacking rather than addition. For example, a finger movement is the outcome of antecedent oscillation(s) for posture and midline motility that partitions to the limb and digits. This is a single act in which an embryo of finger movement is nested as an aim or potential in a system of rhythmic levels for posture and gait.

Evidence for this comes not only from the study of pathology, but from research showing that purposeful finger movements arise at the peak of the cycle of essential or resting tremor. The unconscious nature of the system, with the actor unaware of preparatory phases, has also been confirmed in the widely-cited studies of the readiness potential. This is the case for language, speech, perception, indeed all mentation, as well as creative thought. What arrives in consciousness undergoes a micro-temporal traversal through unconscious phases. If successive phases are simultaneous until discharge, and if superficial levels are individuations of earlier ones, the entire system can be conceived as a set of vibratory levels, i.e. kinetic melodies that fractionate a succession that is prefigured in the whole.

The outcome of this line of thought is that a mind/brain state, consisting of successive phases that specify behavior into spatial (perceptual) and temporal (action) parts, assumes temporal order when it actualizes, at which point the succession can be discerned, as it were, retroactively. The serial potentiality of the event-sequence within the state, or a series of states, lays down temporal order. In the replacement of states, there is passage from one simultaneity to another, giving the appearance of perspectival time out of simultaneity, which recalls Plato's conception of a moving image of eternity. Conscious time-order is a serialization of successive phases in this transition. On this view, insight is "looking-in" on an evanescent "picture" of the all-at-once nature of formative process. This phenomenon, which everyone has experienced to some degree, is a reminder that a focus on the external, and the continuous seriality of behavior, speech, action and passage in the world, ignoring the inner gaze, prevents a deeper understanding of the outgrowth of order from simultaneity, and the origin of subjective time and creativity in unconscious mind.

Contents also come into consciousness primed by those already exteriorized. In many if not most instances, a creative act begins without awareness of the idea. A painter might start with a line on a blank canvas, a writer with a word on an empty sheet of paper. There is no direction, no sense of what comes next, rather a waiting and hopefulness that a work will emerge. Often this is sufficient to prompt further efforts until the work is completed. In such cases, an unconscious idea is activated by token realizations, or through trial and error attempts until something happens that resonates with the conceptual underpinning of the work. Alternatively, the attempt arouses an incomplete or latent concept, with a reciprocal efficacy of conceptual growth and composition. That is, the parts arouse the whole, which, though not fully formed, discharges the parts.

These remarks imply that the solution to the problem of Maury's dream rests in the conscious order of events that are selected or created out of simultaneity. The sequence, a dream or creative idea, "gathered together" in a simultaneous alignment, enables a conscious selection

—a coming-into consciousness—of events in the most plausible sequence. Certainly, this is true for creative thinking, in which the constituents of an idea arise spontaneously and are then arranged in the order that is the most logical (mathematics or science), efficacious (political, rhetorical) or aesthetically pleasing (art), which is not necessarily that of the acquisition or formation of the idea or the succession of virtual constituents in unconscious mind.

The temporal order conforms to the most relevant parameters, e.g. aesthetic values, contextual or meaning-relations, color, form, persuasiveness, or logic, as in a mathematical proof. In dream, events are presented all at once on waking, with the narrative developing according to the most plausible sequence or interpretation. In creative thought, the contents are not consciously selected, i.e. the selection does not originate in consciousness, since they are inaccessible to conscious mind, but, as they become conscious, they are accepted, rejected, appended, postponed or altered, for use immediately or at another time.[52] Sculpting for what is most adaptive refers to what is most suitable or essential; for example, an assimilation of the contents of an idea to a creative aim or circumstance. While there are occasions when the order unfolds without need of alteration, most writers insert, remove, adjust, reverse, relocate or replace segments in a text. All of this points to the unconscious simultaneity of constituents.

In a word, dream is a creative idea compressed to an instant, apprehended in an act of intuition and unpacked sequentially as a microcosm of composition, while insight is an emphatic realization of unconscious thought accentuated by the fullness of the unconscious idea (or dream) and the suddenness of its transition to a conscious level.

The preceding discussion raises questions as to the transition from unconscious to conscious thought. Dream recall or insight to a creative idea is a sudden, brief awareness of an unconscious content or state. Because of the infrequency and impact of this awareness, and its occurrence in powerful or life-

---

[52] This is consistent with Libet's assertion that consciousness mainly exercises a veto power, while microgenetic theory claims the "veto" occurs in the form of constraints throughout the micro-temporal transition.

changing ideas, the topic has been the focus of a good deal of speculation, but the generation of acts and objects out of the shadows into the light occurs every moment of waking life. All conscious experience develops out of unconscious process. This is especially noticeable in speech and action, in that speech develops out of meaning, purposefulness and grammatical knowledge, while other modes of action develop from an implicit aim or plan. Deliberation for acts of cognition is intermittent; most behavior is spontaneous or automatic. It is inconceivable that acts and utterances are organized, planned and implemented solely at a conscious level. Even acts that follow conscious deliberation, when felt as voluntary and decided by the self, are instigated in the unconscious.

In conventional theory, perceptual objects are presumed to impinge on mind from an external locus, with images deposited as memories of the perceptual experience. In contrast to microgenetic theory, in which objects develop over successive phases to finally detach as extra-psychic entities, standard theory postulates that objects are assembled from feature-receptors activated by sense data, either perceived directly or projected back into the world. Microgenetic theory holds that pre-objects resolve unconscious tension at earlier phases, then pass through an implicit phase of choice in which options may or may not be conscious. All acts and objects begin with instinctual drive, pass through implicit choice and desire to imagery and conscious outcomes.[53] The mental image does not become an object; rather, the substrate of the image either deposits the image or is transformed to a perception. In creative thought, some portion of imagery is attenuated. The attenuated development (neoteny) retains the image prior to adaptive

---

[53] For some, like Searle, to say unconscious thought is physiology begs the question of conscious thought, which is also physiology. Why is one physiological state labeled thought, the other not, depending on consciousness? Unless agency, purposefulness and the precursors of deliberation, action, language and perception, are all fully conscious, which is an absurd proposition. More sanguine philosophers such as Collingwood have argued for an unconscious stage of presupposition at the onset of thought. Wittgenstein claimed that thought begins with instinct.

sculpting. This allows for conceptual growth in relation to thought, feeling and memory.

To withdraw from the world and concentrate on an idea, to meditate, to close one's eyes absorbed in thought, accentuates this subliminal phase and avoids hasty objectification. The growth of imagery is aided by inwardness, by thinking on a problem, by learning and experience, even isolation, all of which allow the idea to mature prior to detachment. This is why many artists do not discuss a work in progress, fearful that the idea, if externalized in speech, will be lost to further growth. When the idea reaches a critical mass or a certainty of formulation, its occurrence in dream or its derivation to consciousness becomes possible, if not inevitable. Thus, one approach to the study of creative thought is to focus on the bridge from mind to world and the reflexive awareness of inner states, namely the formative phases in object-development that run parallel to preparatory phases in action, leading from the core of mind to the outer world.

To review, the inner development of a perception, concealed from observation, inferred from experimental study or pathology, originates in drive aided by will and motivated by core beliefs and values. The phase of (verbal, visual) imagery is parsed by sensibility in perceptual cortex, which is the endpoint, not the initial stage, of percept-development. The final image is sculpted to conformity. Adaptive pressures on the outgoing stream partly explain the need for isolation and reduced engagement for many creative people. The abruptness of the transition from a private image to a public object reinforces the belief that objects are outside the percipient subject. From this point of view, creativity and insight will resist explanation unless perception is conceived as going from mind to world, not the reverse. The final object is an objectification of a subjective ground. Dream and creative ideas represent antecedent phases glimpsed in momentary insight or recovered in composition.

At the point of externalization, the major portion of sensibility meets the forming object. The radical adjustment to a three-dimensional space and time-order from an egocentric or dream-like space and non-perspectival time, the shift from a fluid image to a fixed object, from freedom to limitation, from imagination to reality, with recurrence of this traversal every moment of waking life, engraves in mind the belief that thought, though internal, has a relation to the external world, while objects, though mental images positioned in external space, have a relation to the mind.

An object as an independent existent is a sudden, com-pelling fact, though instances of incomplete detachment shed light on this transition. A failure to relinquish the (substrate of the) image in passage to an object gives intermediate forms such as hallucination or eidetic imagery. Psychoactive drugs peel away the veneer of normalcy, reducing the effects of sensibility and uncovering submerged cognition. Psychosis exposes the shift from inner mind to outer world as objects become thoughts and the reverse. Imagery in the context of personal or experiential memory undergoes endogenous growth prior to actualization to account for creative ideation. The retention of the image prevents adaptation and loss of objects. Insight is an immediate apprehension of the image *in statu nascendi*. In the composition of a scientific or artistic work, recurrent actualizations adapt the content to rational mind and the sensory world. Conscious states and contents are an out-come of unconscious process. That is, consciousness is an outcome, a relation that is an endpoint, refreshed each waking moment, not an agency. The feeling of agency is dependent on the state and the content, and is also a relation elaborated within the momentary act. A conscious self does not select unconscious ideas or fragments into consciousness or dream report; rather, the consciousness of dream or idea is a deliverance of unconscious process.

Chapter 10

Self and Creativity

The self navigates between habit and disposition

As previously discussed, in creative activity the self is passive or receptive to ideas that arise without conscious effort. An illustration of this is the unsuccessful search for a name or word that later, after some distraction, pops into the mind. The effort to find the word, like an effort to come up with a creative idea, is counter-productive. Goethe said that thinking doesn't help thought. Deliberation may aid in creative thought, not by arousing ideas, but by maintaining concentration and avoiding distraction.

In some respects, the self in a creative state resembles the self of dream, which is passive to the image content. The withdrawal or isolation that is usually necessary for creativity fosters receptiveness. The release from awareness of the immediate environment alters the entire mental state, which becomes closer to imagery, to a more receptive self and to the experiential memories from which the core self is forged. The relative suspension of agency accompanies the inwardness and lack of intentionality or direction to an external object or object-like states, such as propositions. The self no longer has an object in consciousness, or rather the object field shrinks to the pen and paper with an internal focus excluding all distracting stimuli. In the waking state, one can have volitional feeling for a mental image, since imagery is embedded in conscious perception. Once perception is lost, degraded or reduced, the self does not have an intentional object, and the sense of agency is lost or diminished. Passivity in the act of creation accompanies a cognitive focus on imagination in a retreat from the world, a world that fully disappears in dream. This accounts for the attribution of creativity to a muse or divine inspiration, when receptiveness implies that the self is not felt as the author of its own creations.

Elsewhere, I have argued that the self is a liminal phase through which mental contents develop. The creative self is a coalescence of experiential memories, implicit beliefs and values that together constitute the ground of habitual thought and behavior and the source of character and personality.[54] The core self has privileged access to implicit memorial experience and the ingredients of personality (Fig. 10.1). Early experience becomes the structure of the self. One could say that amnesia for early childhood represents the assimilation of memory to personality, while later memories are in a more superficial relation to the self. The unconscious core is shaped and activated by instinctual drive, passing to the liminal or conscious self, which adapts to the inner and outer situation. The transformation from unconscious to conscious self, anterior to the deposition of mental and external contents, gives the feeling of a self behind its own derivations. The intentionality of a conscious state is a relation between the self and an object or mental content in the context of a complete perceptual development. This content can be a proposition, an image or an object. The feeling of intentionality as a relation across phases in the mental state is tied to consciousness. Except for objectless moods, such as anxiety or depression, the intentional is an invariable attribute of consciousness. The feeling of a relation is actually a relational feeling, in that feeling is the dynamic within and among mental contents. Passivity and agency, though dependent on content, are feelings of a more or less active relation of the core and conscious self to imagery and the world.

---

[54]   See Bricklin (2015) for an insightful account of the views of William James and other philosophers on the self, the relation to meditative states and to the mystical tradition.

External events {

Objects, acts

↑ ↑

Images, desires

Cs mental events {

Conceptual feeling

Empirical self

↑

Ucs events {

Primitive categories

Core self

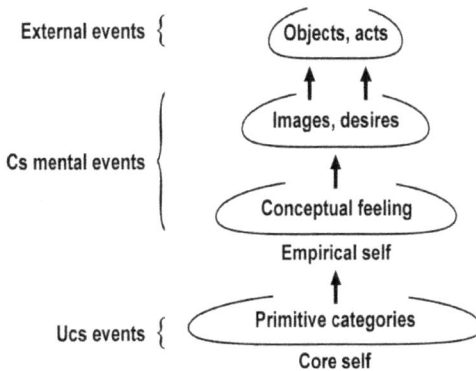

Fig. 10.1: The mind/brain state arises in archaic formations bound up with the unconscious or core self, instinctual drive and drive-categories (drive-representations), passing to the conscious self and conceptual-feeling, finally to acts and objects in the world. Drive-categories enlist implicit values, beliefs and dispositions. Visual and verbal (inner speech) imagery is introspective content in the context of a full object-development; it is not a terminal addition, but an accentuation of penultimate phases. The trajectory from depth to surface is continuous. The final phase of objects is the distal-most phase of mind. The transition is from archaic to recent in distributed brain systems, from self to object, from mind to world, from memory-like to perception-like events, from potential to actual, from past to present and from dream and fantasy to an adaptive resolution. Through a cascade of whole-part or context-item shifts, guided by sensory constraints at successive points, a fully subjective transition objectifies a perceptual world. The entire sequence—the absolute mental state—is an indivisible epoch that perishes on completion and is revived, in overlapping waves, in a fraction of a second.

When the object dominates the mental state without an intermediate phase of introspection or imagery, i.e. when action and attention go immediately to the world, passivity in relation to the object reaches the point where the image no longer belongs to the self and is felt as an independent perception. Detachment leaves the self behind, as the object enters another world. This is the peak of receptiveness. The image passes from an extra-personal but still mental space to a space that is extra-psychic and perceived as physical. The central point is that the object and its external space, however real they seem, are a creation of the mind. When incomplete pre-objects externalize, such as hallucinations, they carry with them attributes of the psychic that conflict with externality. Hallucination may seem real, but not object-like in its realness. If the entire field is hallucinatory, whether a dream or an hallucinatory psychosis, hallucination is no longer felt as having originated in mind. The feeling of real-ness differs from reality, which is not felt but inferred. Realness is in the collusion of the perceptual modalities, as in waking and in dream, when more than one perceptual modality is entrained and the false realness of the image cannot be discon-firmed. In a word, the object, which is presumed to be the start-ing point of perception in standard theory, is the final phase in microgenesis, with sensibility trimming the psyche of mal-adaptive or irrelevant qualities (Fig. 10.1).

When certain mental contents attract attention in a per-ceptual state, agency or activity in relation to the image gives a feeling of voluntary control. This tends to occur for an image closer to the world, such as an eidetic or imagination image, e.g. picturing a mouse crawling on the back of an elephant. When in dream the object disappears, the self is passive to an imagery that is extra-personal but not extra-psychic. The receptive self of dream resembles the passive self in creative thought more than the active self of ordinary experience. The greater proximity to the inner life in creative thought facilitates richness and possibility, bringing the dominant focus of cog-nition away from objects and closer to thought and imagery.

The self is agent and recipient of its own creative ideas. As an agent, it is the author of the work; as a recipient, the idea is felt as an inheritance. But anyone who works in a creative way understands that agency, or deliberate action, provides the con-ditions for creativity, i.e. the setting, the preparation, the tools, the privacy or reclusiveness, the discipline, but after that, there is a concentrated waiting, a not always fruitful expectation of a creative visitation. The lack of agency for a creative idea is supported by the sense that the work is a gift that may not be repeated, thus the common anxiety that the work, once completed, may not be followed by another.

The experiential self, or the self in relation to personal memory, or more precisely a self that is formed of experiential memories that are usually irretrievable, is often plumbed by an artist for the material of a work. Many search for the genuine self, and a writer, more than most, wants to express an authenticity of personal experience, especially in an early novel, where there may be an attempt to recollect, imagine and/or transform events of childhood or adolescence. The exploration of the distant past is like a depth-analysis of the self, of personality and character, allowing the self to "speak" through the art-form, reminiscent of Nabokov's late memoire "Speak, memory." What is revived may not be what is hoped for, or what is genuinely one's own, since what is most essential are the early memories that go into the formation of the self.[55]

Recollection for experience in adolescence or maturity, unlike early memories that are constitutive, is in a more superficial (extrinsic) relation to the self. The self is distinct from later memories, and relates to them as objects or facts. Memories that constitute the self cannot be retrieved and are resistant to recall. In any event, to put it bluntly, what comes up, whether creative or plagiarized, is what the self produces, and the more genuine and honest the creation, no matter the emphasis on fantasy or actuality, the greater the validity, though not necessarily the value, of the work and the deeper the sense of self-discovery. The wider, more varied and learned the experience, the greater the imaginative drift from actuality, the more authentic and less self-referential, the less journalistic, with imagination providing texture to the fabric of the piece; an artist with skill and a unified vision can imbue a concept with personal feeling that touches others beyond the confines of private experience. The significance of receptiveness is that the unconscious does the

---

[55] In this respect, there is a resemblance to cases of amnesia, in which recall may show features of dream. One example is the case of Betlheim and Hartmann (1951), in which an amnesic recalled a story of a violent rape as that of a woman burned in a fire.

writing as opposed to a conscious artifice. Authenticity is ransacked when consciousness and deliberation are fully engaged.

Another attribute of the self essential to a high order of creativity, flexibility during the creative act, imaginatively transposes the artist into the work or into the public mind. In a sense, the artist is a covert actor one step removed from performance, affecting the audience through the medium of the art. Through an attentive engagement, feeling generated in composition is conveyed to, or renewed in, the observer. Emotion also determines topic, ingredients and the means to convey them. If feeling is too weak, the artwork is dry, as in an historical novel or philosophical essay. If too strong, feeling can be disruptive. The self and layers of conceptual feeling adapt content to the world, dissipating feeling as they mitigate excess.

What has been said for artistic creativity is not readily applied to work in science. While art and science have much in common as to insight, unconscious thought and composition, along with some features of personality, e.g. confidence and ambition, scientific creativity requires a sequestration of feeling and exclusion of personal experience. In science, creativity is largely within a profession with problems that limit the field of thought. The self of a creative scientist, philosopher or mathematician may be arrogant, even ruthless, but unlike the case in many artworks, personality is not ingredient in the actual product.[56] For the artist, the challenge is to convey feeling in a given art-form. For the scientist, the problem is to move further in a restricted domain of thought. The scientist wants a solution that, in most instances, will orphan its author as the field moves forward. Only the greatest of scientists, philosophers or mathematicians will be remembered for the depth, range and originality of their thought. Creative work of a lesser order provides the background out of which the exceptional arises. The scientist hopes for great discovery, but most discoveries are absorbed, obsolete and superseded in a few years. In contrast,

---

[56] Most of the Nobelists I have met have been men of strong and aggressive character, which would seem at odds with the passivity and openness necessary for discovery.

the work of the artist is conceived as a finality that, in a gifted individual, is meant to be unique and enduring.

1. Creation and Subjectivity

Though many psychologists and philosophers conceive the mind as a collection of causal objects equivalent to the brain, or for that matter to the outer world, such that the brain is merely a complex physical system that is part of nature's mechanism, with subjectivity absent in objects and presumed eliminated or reducible to brain mechanism, thus also part of physical nature, a subjectivist perspective on mental activity, and by implication nature as well, is essential for an explication of creative thought. Instead of importing the physical world into the mind, microgenetic theory exports mind into the physical world. Mechanical structures in brain and nature are not physical solids but categories invested with thought and value. An image of the physical world is realized in brain, delimited by sense data that make perception possible. On this view, the objective world, as an objectification of the subjective, is in the mind, not outside it, with the physical inferred from the adequacy of perception and the efficacy of action, particularly since the consciousness of acts and objects is off-line with physical passage.

The novelty perceived in a changing world is not the locus of individual creativity, but the instantiation of mind/brain process carried outward into objects. Since objects are categories, not things, and categories realize whole/part relations, change and adaptation in the world represent a lesser order of creativity with respect to magnitude and originality. Ordinarily, we do not believe inanimate objects and lower organisms have an inner life apart from the micro-temporal process through which they actualize. Objects are taken as separate existents in an external world with interaction on their causal surface. However, change, adaptive or not, is in the replacement of an object in the context of a world that is also replaced. The shifting relations among objects, as those within the object itself, are the result of incessant recurrence, perishing and replacement, not superficial impacts. We infer purposeful-ness in behavior in animals that, in man, becomes volitional, but this distinction does not play a major role in ordinary judgments of change and adaptation, only in hesitation at decisional points or when an observer assumes a philosophical attitude. In adaptation or creativity, the greater the quality of innovation, the more thought is engaged, even when action is implemented in a more or less automatic manner.

In a causal world, the perceived interaction of objects is not assimilated to the formative or diachronic process through which they come into momentary existence, nor, for that matter, to the ongoing renewal of the natural world. In the causal model of change, creativity is analogous to a miracle that interrupts the natural order. Nature approaches creative process in evolutionary growth and adaptation. As noted, new growth in evolution arises as a branching of earlier stages in development just as the creative arises at earlier phases in thought. One principle is that reproduction as the measure of adaptation is analogous to recurrence as the basis of sustained existence. Another principle applicable to evolution and creativity is that process develops from the privacy of the preliminary to the publicity of adaptive success. The accentuation of pre-terminal phases in revival is the origin of growth in imaginative form.

The subjective fills the conscious world as an illusory film between a mirror of objective reality that appears infinite in all directions and a physiological unconscious that seems bottomless. Every act of thought passes through the arc of consciousness to a negative image of the real. Art and thought actualize the subjective to objects in public space. When the artwork leaves the mind, it may be perceived as an embodiment of thought or a continuation of the artist's mind, but it is also external to its creator. A word written on paper becomes, for others as for the writer, a physical object. One moment it is private and subjective; the next, public and physical. What are we to make of this transition? How is a thing one moment psychic, perceived the next as physical? If it is plausible that a subjective image becomes a physical entity, it is conceivable that all objects in the physical world precipitate out of subjectivity, indeed, that all nature is the sediment of a universal subjectivity. Either a thought is a physical entity coordinate with a written word, or the word is still a psychic object after it leaves the mind.

Creativity embraces this transition. Instead of mind reduced to brain mechanism, and the creative as emergent, or an accident of neuronal firing, or a rearrangement of nerve impulses, creativity is the manifestation of something original and unexpected effectuated by thought. If a word in the mind corresponds with a physical substrate in the brain, what does the word on paper correspond to? I would say the word as idea and the word as object refer to successive segments in perception, thus successive phases in the mind/brain state. Is it not more consistent to say that subjectivity in the mind objectifies — but remains subjective — in the world, i.e. that image and object are subjective all the way through? The subjective ground of perceptual objects in the world is an instance of the belief that all nature is god's creation. This also explains why the genius, in creating objects out of subjectivity but seemingly *ex nihilo,* is thought to have god-given powers. The act of creation is not just for something original or inspiring, but for the actualization of a novel existent. Because it is a dramatic illustration of the transition from thought to object, from mental image to physical thing,[57] and because of the complexity and/or originality of both thought and product and the mystery of transition from idea to artwork — even the creative thinker is puzzled — creativity shines a light on a process unnoticed in every act of thought.

One way of conceptualizing the shift from inner to outer is in the relation of mental category to physical sensation. An example is the assignment of intermediate acoustic stimuli to neighboring phonemic categories, such as /b/ and /p/, with "deafness" for stimuli transitional in the acoustic spectrum. A common example is the difficulty for Japanese speakers with /r/ and /l/. The same observation applies to the relation of color categories to the physical light spectrum, namely "blind-

---

[57] Lower animals are embedded in their environment with the transition from subject to object and back continuous or without clear boundaries (see discussion in Koenderink, 2015). As the subject-object distinction becomes sharper, the transition from mind to world becomes more obscure.

ness" to transitional stimuli, or their assignment to adjacent categories. These findings confirm that mental categories enfold visual and acoustic sensation, e.g. acoustic stimuli are perceived categorically, not acoustically, without direct correlation of the physical and the psychic. The categorical nature of psyche is primary, delimited by sensibility.

An interpretation in which category/item transitions shaped by sensation underlie the perceptual process differs from the presumption that reception or in-processing of physical data "fills the bins" of empty categories. A receptive theory entails an accumulation of sense data in the construction of categories and/or the establishment of the boundaries of what is perceptible. The microgenetic view is that the categories are foundational, and that items extracted, e.g. phonemes, colors, are themselves categories. The category/member shift is an elicitation within category-boundaries of data that are sub-categories even to the final extraction. With reference to creativity, if the cognitive process is conceptual all the way through, creative thought does not need to generate novel concepts, but expands and, through overlap, propagates concepts that, like brides-in-waiting, are attendant on arousal.

2. Habit, Tradition and Composition

The role of tradition is not dissimilar in art and science, though science, while respecting prior research and methodologies, will occasionally have to ignore the conventions that tradition demands. Art also is constrained by tradition, but is inclined to a rupture with the past and an assertion of individuality. There is a tender balance between the reins of tradition, which establish the tactics, problems, methods and standards, along with the conformity exerted on novelty, and the impulse to break with the past and discover everything fresh and anew. In both, the *Zeitgeist* has a powerful effect. Elsewhere I have addressed this matter, maintaining that mediocrity is not innocuous but pernicious, in that it lowers the public, and even professional, taste for works of inestimable value.

The relevance of tradition is the inculcation through training of ways of doing things in art and science that translate to the mental process underlying creative thought. Tradition as a relatively stable pattern of belief is opposed to change, or at least it informs change so as not to stray too far from consensual facts. Yet tradition, which is central to religion, scholarship and most fields of professional endeavor, can also, in habitual thinking, in timidity or fear of censure, be a powerful brake on creative thought. Tradition, though essential to the "tools" of a trade — skill, style, knowledge, technique — as in the form of a sonata, the rules of perspective, the palette of the painter, is both guarantor and antagonist of originality. When the creative is independent of tradition, there are no guidelines or standards, indeed, no knowledge base that would aid in formulating a novel idea. When the individual is obeisant to received wisdom or praxis, mental process will iterate habitual patterns of thought in slow incremental advance. Genuine creativity occurs when the individual absorbs tradition but goes beyond, reinterprets and/or reformulates tradition in a novel perspective or paradigm.

Most thought, work and conversations tend to be repetitive. People tend to have only a few categories of predictable interaction. Every new encounter is an opportunity to regurgitate the same life story, tell the same tales and jokes, and ask the same questions. People never tire of repeating themselves, showing slight deviation within a category of thought or behavior, essentially saying or doing the same thing over again in different ways. The basis of mind/brain theory in recurrence mandates consistency through iteration; habit engraves recurrence in patterns of behavior and sensory adaptation enforces conformity through elimination of deviance. The combination works to preserve the predictable and make nontrivial originality unusual.

In the mind/brain state, process reinforces patterns of thought and behavior as a deterrent to genuine creativity. Nature is conservative. Adaptation prevents wide disparities within species, encourages routine, and acts as a brake on novelty, promoting the most parsimonious and least innovative solutions to events in the social and physical environment. Within a category such as feeding, there is little variation among organisms within a species. Innovation increases in the ascent to higher animals. The process that accounts for sameness also accounts for originality, the former governed by adaptation, the latter by offshoots at penultimate phases. Scientific creativity also has adaptive value, whether an invention for farming, medicine or weaponry, but creativity in art, apart from its role in magical belief, has little if any evolutionary consequence. The relative freedom from adaptive pressures and the satisfaction of subjective need make creativity in art, mathematics or philosophy a quality that, like consciousness or value, is not explained solely on an evolutionary basis. The effort to create, like that to seek value in a material universe, requires the individual to subvert, exploit or co-opt patterns of recurrence, habit, adaptation and constraint in order to overcome limitations on creativity for personal satisfaction.

These obstacles to the creative explain why an individual who is fortunate enough to have found a theme is reluctant to abandon it. A scientist, regardless of past discoveries, will spend a lifetime in a specialized field. It is the rare individual, e.g. Picasso, Dali, who is creative in different styles and/or media. Even those who are not creative may find enough satisfaction in a hobby, reading, gardening, the work of others to sustain an interest throughout life to the exclusion of creative attempts. These iterative pursuits affirm the control on creative derailment by recurrence, habit and the influence of consistency. There are, of course, many ways to be creative other than art and science. We all know people of high spirit, intelligence, wit, a varied experience and an engaging personality, of whom we might say that creativity has gone into their life, not their work. While the conversation of an artist or scientist is often as banal as that of an untalented public, now and then one meets a person for whom conversation is an art-form exclusive of other artistic pretentions. As Oscar Wilde remarked, the man who can dominate a London dinner-table can dominate the world. Wit is a limited, almost fragmentary, form of creativity in conversation. In this respect, one thinks of Wittgenstein's sarcastic attack on cleverness as an obfuscation of thought.

From the standpoint of mental process, tradition can be viewed as the background from which creativity arises, essential to the maturing scientist or artist, not only for technique and a sense of what has been done before, but for challenges, opportunities, standards and what needs to be accomplished. In the form of habit, tradition assimilated to the native endowment exposes topics and problems to which creativity is addressed, but in the mental state a path molded by the habitual establishes limits on what can arise and what is acceptable, much as a river shapes its banks and in turn is shaped by them. Moreover, once a theme is found, or played out repeatedly in artworks or scientific research, it comes to consume the individual, who, having struggled to find a voice and wishing to go on to new work or discovery, now struggles to suppress it.

Thus a central problem for the effects of tradition on thought concerns the overcoming of established trends for original discovery, and the overcoming of personal history for further creation, especially in another — adjacent or unrelated — field. The first form of habit is related to immersion in the products of others, the second grows endogenously. One might refer to extrinsic and intrinsic habit, or experience acquired by instruction and exposure and experience acquired through dedication. Having attained knowledge of a field, it is necessary to avoid customary thinking to accomplish something original. Then, in those who have made significant contributions, it is necessary to unlearn a body of knowledge to set out in a new direction. Indeed, at a certain point in life it may be unclear to the creative person whether the difficulty starting out in another field is due to a sluggish imagination, inability to acquire sufficient knowledge and fluency late in life, auto-didacticism or indoctrination by past ideas and experience that infects original undertakings. Discovery is difficult enough in the first place but faces additional obstacles the second time around. A discovery or artistic gift that is first a possession becomes a pattern of thought that possesses the thinker.

The genius is bound to the ordinary, but not reduced to it, in sharing a common process, but genius expands the ordinary beyond the normal limit. The process that accounts for a large brain accounts for a larger one. The process of thought in everyday life is the same process as in genius. Memory and imagination may be simple or rudimentary in one person and fertile in another, but the same process is involved. Giftedness, like pathology, exposes what is concealed. The few categories of thought, behavior and conversation allotted to the average individual in the day-to-day routine of life also apply to the artist and scientist, though within each category there is greater knowledge, depth and flexibility. What the layman or genius does at 30 may not be so different at 60; increasing skill, fluency, confidence, success or self-satisfaction and fear of being a dilettante reinforce ingrained tendencies stoked by recurrence. This common observation is a confirmation of uniformity in mental process. Creativity in concert with other aspects of nature and nurture is not a unique frame of mind or mental process, but an exceptional development or exploitation of certain features of universal process.

3. Ideation and Formulation

The notion that an inspired idea comes more or less complete, with composition eliciting the details, though it may relevant to a painting, sculpture or brief verse, or the solution of a scientific problem, seems less pertinent to artistic works of some magnitude, where a general theme or an awareness of the topic and content of a lengthy work, a novel, a symphony, a large fresco or architectural work is not, I would think, despite anecdotal reports, presented in sufficient detail for the artist to "read off" the idea in repeated acts of composition. The apperception of a two-dimensional image or static design seems indisputable. Accomplished painters have described to me a sudden, comprehensive and detailed vision of the whole of a painting, usually in a dreamy state or during relaxation. I believe the difficulty in a comparison to a complex temporal sequence, as in music or literature, can be resolved in the simultaneity of unconscious ideation, which makes a temporal sequence equivalent to a spatial image.

There is the foundational idea and the specific contents or subsidiary ingredients that carry a work to completion. The insight that prompts inspiration recurs in the partition to subcategories with a restricted focus, such as a sequence of variations on a musical theme, or the next paragraph or chapter in a novel. In comparison to the totality of the initial insight, continuous partition yields a fraction of the impact and immediacy of the original idea, which is revived with diminished vivacity, as a background that generates the ingredients through which the work is fully actualized. In a novel, every line contributes to the originality of the whole, though in isolation the fragment may have little creative impact. Every word or phrase, every note or measure that surfaces to consciousness is assessed as to fitness or expressiveness to the overarching theme. The demand on micro-creativity in execution depends on the original insight much as a structural element in an architectural design depends on a conception of the whole, each element a fillip for others by propagation or by arousal of the background idea.

Usually, one sets out on a book as on a voyage, knowing the origin and destination but uncertain how to get from here to there or what happens in between. For example, in writing this essay, there is a clear impression of overall intent and a vaguer idea of exactly how to implement it. In large part this depends on having the confidence that subsidiary ideas and words will arise as they are needed. There can be uncertainty over a section, a paragraph or a word, but what survives is what feels right in a given context, and this feeling of rightness, which relates the conscious data to unconscious phases of word-sound, relevance and meaning, accompanies revision, elimination and eventual satisfaction. The recognition that a word is not quite right, or using it as a place-marker until a better one is found, or the sense it needs to be revised, unpacked or supplemented, are conscious perceptions similar to those of a careful reader. Some artists depend on an editor, colleague or friend to parse excess or improve word choice. T.S. Eliot gave the manuscript for *The Waste Land* to Ezra Pound, who crafted it into a masterpiece.

In all fine works, the choice of part-concepts, words and phrases comes from subtle relations to underlying context, for which the writer has a feeling of contact but little direct access. The search for the best continuation or implementation is accompanied by a feeling of agency that informs the choice, which is accepted or vetoed. Through this process, the idea pours out words that may be perfectly apt or mere approximations, but eventually, if the author's hopes are fulfilled, they will realize the original intent. This process, in which every part resonates with the whole, is iterated every moment in creative work. The macro is implemented over time as the inciting idea shapes micro-ingredients that bring it to fruition. For the gifted writer, the theme finds satisfaction in recurrent salvos, each fulfilling a need implicit in the idea behind it.

Consider the title of Milan Kundera's novel, *The Unbearable Lightness of Being*, which is both a literary and philosophical work. While it is not possible, in the choice of this title, to know the mind of the author—especially unconscious sources—the intent is to allude to themes such as love, sex and eternal return. For me, there is charm in the incompatibility of the words reminiscent of Chomsky's "colorless green ideas", a phrase that is grammatical but contradictory, e.g. green is not colorless, ideas are not green, and so on. Here, lightness is not ordinarily unbearable, and being evokes substance, not lightness. I do not know whether this was intentional or fortuitous, but the beauty of the work is enhanced in the title by a kind of accidental poetry, possibly representing conflict, ambiguity or bi-perspectivalism. A major work of art rarely discloses its full meaning even to the author, who is at the mercy of unconscious ideas stirring to actuality and to which he is largely a vehicle of expression.

In this account, in which the transition from macro to micro partitions the whole to a multiplicity of parts, what is clear is that the whole—the idea, concept or theme of a work, a problem or a discovery—is a category that may present as a brief vivid image, with the parts sub-categories of actual data in a scientific or artistic product. A sentence in a novel realizes a concept or sub-category implicit in the whole; each line, measure or figure can be thought of as a category to its elements (words, notes, colors), which in turn can be conceived as more restricted concepts. The partition is not from a single whole to many parts, but from wider to narrower categories or fields, in which the actual data of the work, though externalized, can still be conceived as a sub-category.

For example, in the preceding sentence, the word "conceived" is a member of a lexical category and could be replaced by "taken", "interpreted", "conceptualized", "thought of", "viewed", "expressed" and so on, each with a slightly different meaning, while the final selection evokes subsidiary possibilities. Conceived implies "thought of", not "expressed"; it points to the inner life and is an appeal to the reader. Conceived is less emphatic than "is", and connotes hesitation, diffidence or uncertainty, though from my perspective the tenuous quality of the word is aligned with the theoretical and provisional nature of this work. There is also sensitivity to the prior use of the word, not only to avoid repetition, but also for uniformity of context, all of which, in spite of the feeling of agency, is largely unconscious and automatic.

Chapter 11

Feeling

Feeling points the direction that reason wants to go

For microgenetic theory, feeling is pervasive in thought and action; it is ingredient in object development, undergoing transformation in the passage from the core of mind to its externalized surface, *from unconscious drive through conscious desire to object worth*. It suffuses concepts as an affective tonality, whether the powerful feelings of instinctual drive, the focused emotions of love, fear, hate and desire, the subtle feelings of affect ideas (pride, envy, etc.), or the externalized feelings of object value or worth. Feeling distributes into the emotions that are felt and conveyed in speech, expressed in poetry, music and song, or mediated by painting, sculpture, architecture and other art forms. A central thesis of this theory is that feeling and concept (or object) do not come together in association, but are unified *ab origine*. Every concept or category has an affective quality and every feeling has a conceptual frame. Feeling as becoming is what realizes process. Objects as being realize concepts. The transition of feeling over phases accompanies the formative history of acts and objects. Becoming deposits being in the actualization of entities, organisms or mental states. This account of feeling informs the approach to art and science.

In science or philosophy, emotion does not appear to enter the work, reinforcing the ideal of rational concepts independent of feeling. Conversely, it is believed that animal drives or intense human emotions — panic, rage — do not realize concepts (categories). These erroneous ideas have been fully addressed in the cited references. The common view is that affect is decanted, displaced or "left behind" in the formation of scientific or philosophical concepts. In other words, abstract or technical ideas are not thought of as having an affective charge; they are conceived as mental solids available for commentary by others, distinct from the emotional state of the thinker. Feeling may be anterior to the work as anticipation or motivation, incidental to the work as excitement, or follow the work as pride or satisfaction, but a hint that feeling, other than a hunch or an intuition, is intrinsic to the work, or plays a role in (the content of) philosophical argument, in mathematical logic or in research studies and their interpretation, is usually enough to raise doubts about the results.

However, an affective element is clearly present in abstract concepts, such as the common bias, as Popper wrote, in the effort to confirm an hypothesis rather than refute it or, as is generally the case, to ignore views and arguments not supportive of the principal thesis. It is inarguable that scientific studies often disregard data or opinions outside a dominant paradigm, choosing only those observations that re-affirm their conclusions. The neglect of competing ideas is not necessarily due to a rational choice of the most promising line of study; more often it represents a deliberate blindness or neglect in which a coterie of like-minded colleagues are complicit. There is a great deal invested in a given line of inquiry: funding, reputation and so on. Generally, science progresses slowly, due to the need for confirmation and the weight of a consensus that supports positive findings and eliminates those that are negative or reflect an alternative line of inquiry. The effect, whether or not justified, is to carry what began as an emotional bias into an unshakeable conviction. The provisional in science gives way to unquestioned certainty in supposedly affect-free beliefs.

The covert feeling in scientific concepts is assumed to be extrinsic to the data, just as the feeling in philosophical concepts is considered irrelevant to the argument, or as the morality of an artist or philosopher is irrelevant to his works; yet feeling is essential in art and, for the most part, is meant to be implicit in the content. Feeling is perceived as localized in the artwork and somehow conveyed, by means of the art, from the artist to others. A moment's reflection, however, will disclose that the actual work, e.g. figures, words, shapes, lines, colors, contrasts, tones, is a set of features or contrasts that, like a sunset, have the capacity to arouse feeling but do not contain it. Still, we tend to think that the artwork "houses" the feeling that went into its creation, and that feeling is transported from the artist to the work, which may or may not be the case, and then from the work to the observer, in whom, it is argued, a deep understanding or sympathetic identification can revive the feeling that went into its composition.

Art designed to elicit feeling, rather than convey it, is inauthentic or manipulative. The feeling may reflect technical mastery or, on a psychological basis, a compensatory reaction in someone who is otherwise dispassionate. Many artists and philosophers are loathsome individuals, yet strike a lofty tone in their work. An artwork, like a philosophy, may complement or mirror the personality and, by inference, the emotional state of its author. In art, Dali, a bit of a fraudulent genius, is an example, considering that Freud told him his paintings were misrepresentations of the unconscious. In philosophy, Schopenhauer is an example of the influence of a morbid personality on presumably affect-free thought. Whitehead asked, if philosophy were truly an exercise in purely rational thought, why is there so much argument and bickering?

In contemporary science, personal feeling tends to be distilled in the interdisciplinary nature of research. While the genius no doubt continues to work in relative isolation, more often confined to theory, the drudgery of experimental research requires a team of indentured servants, i.e. students, along with experts in neighboring fields to give heft to the conclusions. The director of a research group is usually a highly productive individual, like the CEO of a corporation, who leads and inspires, raises funds and travels the lecture circuit, spreading the gospel of the lab. A plethora of conferences creates a constant demand for novel results, such that a research facility is like a factory for scientific data. Most individuals who direct such labs, even minor celebrities in their field, though capable enough, are still of modest ability compared to great men of the past, and their work, with the exception of a rare breakthrough, is soon forgotten. Such individuals have a strong character and competitive streak, which is essential for a middling talent to succeed, but in scientific and technical fields, feeling and personality are, in principle, outside the finished work.

Although scientific discovery or the products of abstract thought, apart from the "extrinsic" emotions discussed above, are presumed in the ideal to be untainted by intrinsic feeling, one can agree that, at least in one respect, feeling in scientific, philosophical or mathematical work is similar to that in art, namely in value and beauty. Value is both internal and external; it is what informs belief and desire and, as an outreach of feeling that accompanies acts and objects, it is what determines fact and worth. Value traces back to drive, e.g. what determines the objects of predation and sexuality, but it may be felt in the object, e.g. a beloved, a pet, a possession. In science, consensus dissipates personal value as objects become settled facts, but they retain, in existence, realness and worth, a trickle of the feeling that went into their development.

A theory, a discovery or an experiment of sufficient depth and originality has some quota of beauty in aesthetic judgment, one not based on reason but on feeling. The sense of beauty is largely an intuition of the power of an idea or solution to a problem that has long vexed others, particularly when its simplicity is out of proportion to the complexity it explains, or when it seems obvious after it is discovered. Einstein's equation for energy and Darwin's theory of evolution are examples. In abstract concepts, beauty is close to elegance. In addition to formal properties, this includes the solution to a complex problem by one or a few principles.

The elegance of a theory or discovery lies in the simplicity with which complexity is resolved. This implies an essentiality with wide application and without adventitious detail. A multiplicity of fact and observation are explained by a common principle, rule or law. The relation of the simplicity of an explanation to the enormity of what is explained is that of locality to generality, or specificity to universality. In the domain of mind/brain theory, the diversity of normal and pathological behavior can be explained by a law governing qualitative whole/part shifts, which constitutes a fundamental theory of mind/brain. The power of a theory to explain complex and/or diverse phenomena, or the relation of locality to generality, is one facet of the feeling of the sublime (see below). Many can appreciate the beauty of an artwork, but only someone with deep knowledge can appreciate the beauty of a mathematical proof or philosophical argument. The more abstract the concept, the more elusive the feeling. In saying that a mathematical idea or scientific theory is beautiful or elegant, the reference is to perfection at a level rarified by abstraction.

In art, beauty in the classical sense is an attractiveness that depends, *inter alia,* on felicity, form, gracefulness and coherence. Beauty in the elegance of a theory is in parsimony, structure and coherence. This is similar to an artwork, e.g. the depth, insight and nuance of a literary work or the sustained power of a philosophical argument. The judgment of beauty is a feeling that is felt in the creator and the appraiser but like object-value or worth it is assigned to the product. An appraisal based on feeling or intuition cannot be readily explicated on rational grounds. A diamond is appraised for its economic worth and is precious for sentimental reasons, but its beauty seems located in the stone. The infiltration of an object by feeling, the sense of beauty or its approximation in works of creative power, with technical or abstract concepts privileged in that, in ordinary circumstances, they do not flow into objects, accounts for the elusiveness of feeling in scientific or mathematical ideas.

In contrast to technical discovery in which beauty as elegance represents feeling in abstractness, feeling in artworks is more intense and recognizable as an emotion that can be felt and described. In art, when feeling is subtle and/or not immediately felt, as in abstract art, beauty and value still figure as prominently as in scientific or philosophical studies. In most forms of pictorial or representational art, less rarified feelings, e.g. emotions, affect-ideas, are transmitted through the artwork. One can be moved to tears by a Brahms adagio, shaken with joy by the beats of popular dance, feel terror in a painting by Edvard Munch, and grief in an elegiac poem.

Much has been written of feeling in music. Among others, the philosopher Peter Kivy has raised the central question of how acoustic noise induces profound emotion. One approach to this problem is that music captures drive-based feelings associated with phases in action and perception. Feeling is directional (irreversible) energy elaborated over oscillatory levels that correspond to growth planes in forebrain evolution.[58] In the derivation of feeling over levels, early phases correspond to the insistent, rhythmic, repetitive beat of primitive music and the irresistibility of dance or movement. This illustrates the parasitic [symbiotic?] relation of music and language to the action system. Movement is aroused because music entrains the same system over which action unfolds. In primitive or much popular music in which there is a repetitive beat often associated with rhythmic dance, it is likely that the more primeval the sound, the earlier the levels in mind/brain, which recur without partition or propagation at more individuated phases. These earlier levels predominate in the harmonies of chant, also highly repetitive, e.g. the music of Sufism and its motor analog in dervishes. In Buddhist chant, the bass is accentuated along with vocalizations of a guttural type. Such music induces hypnotic states that are conducive to religious worship or spiritual contact. The relation of music to language discussed above in terms of vibratory levels, though outside the scope of this monograph, is an opening that should be explored in greater detail.

1. The Sublime

The concept of the sublime has undergone some change over the centuries. For Edmund Burke, the sublime referred to excitement in the idea of pain and danger, especially the feeling of awe and terror. The sublime is not in the object, but in the mind that apprehends the object. Thus, being eaten by a shark would not qualify as a sublime experience, but the contemplation of death was one of Burke's examples. This account differs from present day usage to describe an object of beauty or a feeling of pleasure, in which the sublime is attributed to the object or pleasurable experience, not the idea of it. Most authors view the beautiful as distinct from the sublime, in that it lacks

---

[58] Whitehead (1938) wrote that "the energetic activity considered in physics is the emotional intensity entertained in life."

the capaciousness or immensity that is part of this experience. Beauty is bounded and finite, and is ordinarily not a source of fear or awe. Further, the sublime is not an object but a response to it, especially a sense of danger. The comparison to something incomprehensibly grand or immense beyond the imagination, especially awe-inspiring events in nature and its infinite expanse, is a persistent theme, especially for the Romantic poets and philosophers.

From this brief summary we can extract, as essential to the sublime, a feeling of awe at the power, the danger and immensity of nature as a relation of mind to the limitless and overwhelming. In contrast to reason, as emphasized in Kant, the sublime depends on a near-ineffable feeling of this relation. Its objects may be beautiful, such as a spectacular vista or landscape, or terrifying, such as a hurricane or thunderstorm. One says a work of art is sublime or "sublimely beautiful" but the feeling is not in the art; it is evoked by the content. A difference in scale or spatial relation figures prominently. Conceivably, the experience derives from a primitive sense of frailty in a solitary and vulnerable individual at the mercy of undomesticated wildness.

An artwork can represent the individual as a locus of subjectivity in the immensity of an objective nature, evoking an intense feeling of the locality of the here and now against the immeasurable vastness of space and everlasting time. The sublime can be felt in the tenuousness of life and the evanescence of beauty—a speck of human existence, the triviality of meaning, purpose and human qualities—in relation to a universe of overwhelming power and indifference. While the spatial relation in life and art dominates, the temporal is felt in musical works in the contrast of an intense living emotion against the cold emptiness of the universe. The sublimity of a late quartet of Beethoven awakens a feeling of mortality, one's own and the composer's, compared to the callous silence of death, or the melancholy passage of a brief personal triumph in the incessant decay of time-eternal.

It is possible, for a select few, to experience the sublime in the profound truth of a mathematical or philosophical theory that resolves a complex problem of universal concern. We may think of a theory, especially in physics, as an object in human thought that lights up the interminable darkness of time and space, a moment of inspired humanity in a material universe. This occurs mostly in life experience but also in art, possibly in science but in theory rather than practice. The sublime entails an idea that touches on a deep truth or, if personal feeling, that of loneliness and wonder, the brevity and fragility of existence, beauty as a subjective moment in unending time and infinite space, or meaning in a world without signification, or the individual spirit in relation to the numinous, like the flickering beacon of a lighthouse in a gigantic storm, or the point of a conscious present in a totality of nothingness, an act of kindness in the "tooth and claw" of nature, the miracle of life and its annihilation in a brute insensate universe.

I have speculated on the nature of the sublime as a sudden, fleeting apprehension of the relation between a point in space or a moment in time set against infinity and eternity. The essential state for the sublime is a simultaneous consciousness of the local and the universal, a point in space, a moment in time in relation to the unfathomable of which it is part. The relation of spatial and temporal locality or their analog to the infinite of space and eternal in time is also a relation of a spatial or temporal part to an encompassing whole. The part/whole relation, for example in the subject/predicate or category/item relation of thought, magnified in creativity, expands to its limits in a momentary mental state. The locus of onset of the mental state, together with the psychic world it elaborates, the fragility of the self in the immensity of space, the passage of the now in eternal duration, the illusory felt as vividly real — these are essential conditions for the experience of the sublime.

The whole generates the parts, but the part is the nucleus of mind in relation to the whole as an expanse of space and the present as a duration in timelessness. The part that is the core elaborates the world that is the whole. The immensity and multiplicity of nature as the outermost reach of mind trace back to the animal inheritance as the progenitor of the self, naked and fearful as an animal in the wild, gazing on oceans vast, the evening sky, mountains without end, solitude, frailty, consciousness and human feeling as a span from self to world, from life to death, to the grandeur the self creates and by which it is subdued.

2. Decline

When young, those we admire and emulate are idealized parents or accomplished others. Having passed through a creative life, the model is then the self of yesteryear, not the aspirations of youth, success and failure, but the disparity of then to now. At some point, unless illness or infirmity intervenes, a decision is made to stop or persevere. If the latter, work will be unsatisfying. Take Wordsworth, who, in later years, for lack of inspiration, revised *The Prelude*, though the youthful version remains the best. We retain the spirit if not the means for a creative life once creativity has passed. The drive is strong, a life-giving force. An artist unable to create is metaphorically dead, as a woman past child-bearing is evolutionarily redundant. What is the consolation of wisdom without the power to artfully convey it? What the worth of songs unsung? The challenge to decline is not to exercise mind in futilities but to profit from what remains. Teaching — imparting knowledge to innocents — has a corrosive effect in stories retold each season. When the soil is fallow, sowing the same seeds will not bring a new harvest.

As they age, many artists repeat a theme with minor variations. Scientists persist in the same research, satisfied with trivial advance. A compensation for decline may be a rigidity of thought with a focus on one idea instead of many. Does inflexibility penetrate more deeply in philosophical speculation by fixing on the essential and mitigating the adventitious? Can perseveration on a topic be perseverance on a theme? If rigidity and limited propagation enhance depth and focus they are rudely offset by the inability to fall into a topic, lose the world and plumb the depths. Perhaps the reservoir of acquired knowledge overwhelms possibilities, or novelty is trumped by technique, or the facility of long-held views deflates spontaneity. In youth, the spring of creativity bubbles over. In age, one has to dig the well.

Another byproduct of normal aging that can earn respect as well as consternation is prolixity or talkativeness. Elders are repositories of history and legend — the oral history of life and culture — the storytellers in a community. But these are handed-down tales, not creative narratives. Linguists who attribute this to verbosity or garrulousness merely describe the behavior without explaining it. Perhaps this too is a sign of iteration and "vertical" thinking at the expense of propagative thought. In spite of a tendency to fixate on a topic—old stories, a scientific program, a philosophical theme—what matters is not wading in shallow waters but plunging in for bounties invisible at the surface.

George Eliot wrote that the sunshine of far-off years lives in us and transforms our perceptions into love. After passing through an artistic life and coming out the other side, most people would say love for family and close friends is all that really counts. The feeling that went into striving and a full creative life now finds an outlet in the simple pleasures of affection and family. Life forces us to accept the roles that aging demands, even if we are unfit to assume them. With loss, a decline to the ordinary is demoralizing; without resignation it leads to despair. Alcohol is a common emollient.

There is no lamentation among the masses for the absence of a creativity they have never known, no more than the color-blind miss colors they have never seen. The world seems divided into those who write and those who read, those who create and those who appreciate. Hegel said he had only one student who understood, and he misunderstood. The gifted are aware of the difference. Indeed, it is brought home in an occasion of writer's block. The masses are the reverse of the congenitally-blind who receive the gift of sight and become profoundly depressed. They are content without a gift they should never have received. Most people adapt to limitations which the creative go beyond. A descent from the peak of genius to the valley of mediocrity is a living death, and only a heart that is strong but foolhardy struggles to regain the heights.

References

Arbib, M. (ed.) (2013) *Language, Music, and the Brain*, Cambridge, MA: MIT Press.

Bergson, H. (1911) *Creative Evolution*, Mitchell, A. (English trans.), London: Macmillan.

Bernstein, N. (1967) *The Coordination and Regulation of Movements*, London: Pergamon.

Betlheim, S. & Hartmann, H. (1951) On parapraxes in the Korsakow psychosis, in Rapaport, D. (ed.) *Organization and Pathology of Thought*, pp. 288–310, New York: Columbia University Press.

Bricklin, J. (2015) *The Illusion of Will, Self, and Time: William James' Reluctant Guide to Enlightenment*, Albany, NY: SUNY Press.

Brown, J.W. (1997) Process and creation, in Anderson, A. & Sahlin, N.-E. (eds.) *The Complexity of Creativity*, Dordrecht: Kluwer.

Brown, J.W. (1998) Foundations of cognitive metaphysics, *Process Studies*, 27, pp. 79–92.

Brown, J.W. (1999) On aesthetic perception, *Journal of Consciousness Studies*, 6, pp. 244–261.

Brown, J.W. (2008) The inward path: Mysticism and creativity, *Creativity Research Journal*, 20, pp. 365–375.

Brown, J.W. (2010) Simultaneity and serial order, *Journal of Consciousness Studies*, 17, pp. 7–40.

Brown, J.W. (2012) *Love and Other Emotions*, London: Karnac.

Brown, J.W. (2014) Mind and brain: A contribution from microgenetic theory, *Journal of Consciousness Studies*, 21, pp. 54–73.

Brown, J.W. (2015) *Microgenetic Theory and Process Thought*, Exeter: Imprint Academic.

Campbell, D. (1960) Blind variation and selective retention in creative thought as in other knowledge processes, *Psychological Review*, 67, pp. 380–400.

Cloots, A. (2000) The metaphysical significance of Whitehead's creativity, *Process Studies*, 30, pp. 36–54.

Cobb, J. (2008) *Whitehead Word Book*, Claremont, CA: P & F Press.

Cytovic, R. (1989) *Synesthesia: A Union of the Senses*, New York: Springer.

Deacon, T. (2011) *Incomplete Nature*, New York: Norton.

Dewan, E. (1976) Consciousness as an emergent causal agent in the context of control systems theory, in Globus, G. et al. (eds.) *Consciousness and the Brain*, New York: Basic Books.

Ebbeson, S. (1984) Evolution and ontogeny of neural circuits, *Behavioral Brain Sciences*, 7, pp. 321–366.

Eccles, J. (1970) *Facing Reality*, Berlin: Springer.

Emmet, D. (1985) *The Effectiveness of Causes*, Albany, NY: SUNY Press.

Emmet, D. (1990) Creativity and the passage of nature, in Rapp, F. & Wiehl, R. (eds.) *Whitehead's Metaphysics of Creativity*, Albany, NY: SUNY Press.

Freud, S. (1966ed.) *Standard Edition*, London: Hogarth Press.

Gardner, H. (1983) *Frames of Mind*, New York: Basic Books.

Garland, W. (1983) The ultimacy of creativity, in Ford, L. & Kline, G. (eds.) *Explorations in Whitehead's Philosophy*, pp. 212–238, New York: Fordham University Press.

Guillford, J. (1980) Some changes in the structure of the intellect model, *Educational and Psychological Measurement*, 48, pp. 1–4.

Hanlon, R. (ed.) (1991) *Cognitive Microgenesis*, New York: Springer-Verlag.

Hartmann, E. von (1893) *Philosophy of the Unconscious*, London: Kegan Paul.

Hebb, D.O. (1949) *The Organization of Behavior: A Neuropsychological Theory*, New York: Wiley.

Hofstadter, D. (1997ed.) *The Love Affair as a Work of Art*, New York: Farrar, Straus and Giroux.

Irvine, W. (2015) *Aha*, New York: Oxford University Press

Jackendoff, R. & Lerdahl, F. (1983) *A Generative Theory of Tonal Music*, Cambridge, MA: MIT Press.

James, W. (1899) *Principles of Psychology*, Boston, MA: Holt.

Janik, A. & Toulman, S. (1996ed) *Wittgenstein's Vienna*, Chicago, IL: Elephant.

Kaufman, J. & Sternberg, R. (2010) *The Cambridge Handbook of Creativity*, Cambridge: Cambridge University Press.

Koenderink, J. (2015) Ontology of the mirror world, *Gestalt Theory*, 37, pp. 119–140.

Koestler, A. (1964) *The Act of Creation*, New York: Macmillan.

Kounios, J. & Beeman, M. (2015) *The Eureka Factor*, New York: Random House.

Kris, E. (1962) *Psychoanalytic Explorations in Art*, New York: IUP.

Kuhn, T. (1962) *The Structure of Scientific Revolutions*, Chicago, IL: University of Chicago Press.

Lashley, K. (1951) The problem of serial order in behavior, in Jeffress, L. (ed.) *Cerebral Mechanisms in Behavior*, New York: Wiley.

Leclerc, I. (1990) Whitehead and the dichotomy of rationalism and empiricism, in Rapp, F. & Wiehl, R. (eds.) *Whitehead's Metaphysics of Creativity*, pp. 1–20, Albany, NY: SUNY Press.

Levitan, D. (2007) *This is Your Brain on Music*, New York: Penguin.

Lewin, K. (1948) *Resolving Social Conflicts*, New York: Harper.

Lewis, D. (1986) *Philosophical Papers*, vol. II, New York: Oxford University Press.

Libet, B. (1985) Unconscious cerebral initiative and the role of conscious will in voluntary action, *Behavioral and Brain Sciences*, 8, pp. 529–566.

Lowes, J. (1927) *The Road to Xanadu: A Study in the Ways of the Imagination*, New York: Houghton Mifflin.

Martin, J. (1972) Rhythmic (hierarchical) versus serial structure in speeech and other behaviors, *Psychological Review*, 79, pp. 487–509.

McTaggart, J.M. (1934/1968) *Philosophical Studies*, New York: Books for Libraries Press.

Mehta, V. (1963) *Fly and the Fly Bottle*, New York: Penguin.

Michon, J., Pouthas, V. & Jackson, J.L. (1988) *Guyau and the Idea of Time*, Amsterdam: Royal Netherlands Academy.

Patel, A. (2008) *Music, Language, and the Brain*, New York: Oxford University Press.

Paul, E. & Kaufman, S. (2014) *The Philosophy of Creativity*, Oxford: Oxford University Press.

Rapp, F. (1990) Whitehead's concept of creativity and modern science, in Rapp, F. & Wiehl, R. (eds.) *Whitehead's Metaphysics of Creativity*, pp. 70–93, Albany, NY: SUNY Press.

Runco, M. & Albert, R. (2010) Creativity research: A historical view, in Kaufman, J. & Sternberg, R. (eds.) *The Cambridge Handbook of Creativity*, Cambridge: Cambridge University Press.

Russell, B. (1948) *Human Knowledge*, New York: Simon and Schuster.

Schilder, P. (1951) On the development of thoughts, in Rapaport, D. (ed.) *Organization and Pathology of Thought*, pp. 497–518, New York: Columbia University Press.

Silberer, H. (1951) Report on a method of eliciting and observing certain symbolic hallucination phenomena, in Rapaport, D. (ed.) *Organization and Pathology of Thought*, New York: Columbia University Press.

Simonton, D. (1999) *Origins of Genius*, Oxford: Oxford University Press.

Smith, G. (2008) The creative personality: In search of a theory, *Creativity Research Journal*, 20, pp. 383–390.

Von Domarus, E. (1944) The specific laws of logic in schizophrenia, in Kasanin, J. (ed.) *Language and Thought in Schizophrenia*, Berkeley, CA: University of California Press.

Vygotsky, L. (1987ed) *Collected Works*, vol. 1, Rieber, R. & Carton, A. (eds.), pp. 243–285, New York: Plenum Press.

Whitehead, A.N. (1933) *Adventures of Ideas*, Cambridge: Cambridge University Press.

Whitehead, A.N. (1938) *Modes of Thought*, New York: Macmillan.

Zaimov, K., Kitov, D. & Kolev, N. (1969) Aphasie chez un peintre, *Encaphale*, 58, pp. 377–417.

Addendum

Summary of Microgenetic Theory

The approach in this book will no doubt be unfamiliar to most readers but the theory is the outcome of over thirty years of clinical study and philosophical speculation. A central theme is the subject-object relation, which in various guises is the relation of self to world, mind to nature, experience to reality, memory to perception and feeling to mechanism. Every philosophy takes a stance on this problem but it is no less fundamental to psychology, though in the latter epistemology tends to be implicit in method and bias. My early work in neuropsychology led to a subjectivist or internalist approach but it may be closer to the truth to say the approach was little by little uncovered as the work went on.

Science and psychology tend to an objectivist or externalist view of the same material as the subjectivism of this book, so that some remarks are needed to orient the reader to what is a strikingly different interpretation. Externalism imports objects into the mind and isolates them from their spatial and temporal context. Internalism works with the same data but retains a richness that is often untestable and speculative. Both accounts have ontological implications. For externalism, it is that mental or external objects are substance-like—physical or logical solids. For internalism (and microgenesis), a *becoming* over the temporal extensibility of an object or entity—a rock or mental state—deposits the *being* that the thing becomes.

There is one reality but many doors through which it is apprehended, and each doorway is a perspective that takes the reality it perceives as the true one. For most people the world of perception is the real world. For some, the question is the degree to which mind encroaches on the physical or the degree to which the physical is installed in the mind. The debate is whether a perspective is direct, a subjective appearance, a model or representation, an illusion or false belief. For this writer, knowledge of reality is inferred from its copy or representation. This takes the subjective to its limits. A long tradition of such thinking includes a negation of the real by denying its existence, creating an alternate reality in art or mystical contemplation and retreating to dream, fantasy, even psychosis. The turn from world to mind can rest on *disillusionment*, but it can be a choice as to the kind of life one wishes to live. A life lived resolutely in the mind is no less vibrant than one in the world. The inner life or an intuition of the primacy of the subjective is the starting point of philosophy. In an echo of Descartes, Schelling wrote that "the science of knowledge cannot proceed from anything *objective*, since it actually begins with a general doubt about the reality of the objective."

Transitional phenomena show that a division of mind and world is not as stark as it appears. The bifurcation of nature into two portions, one mental, one physical, is a way of thinking that derives from and supports the distinction of self and other, past and present, feeling and mechanism. The bifurcation dissolves in all-mind or all-nature, eliminating one of its limbs, the physical in idealism, the mental in materialism, the replacement of nature by mind or the removal of mind from nature and brain, restricting subjectivity to pains, after-images and other *qualia* or assuming that consciousness is the last remaining problem before mind can be fully reduced to material brain function.

It is essential to regain the full scope and character of subjectivity to understand the relation of mind to nature. The first step is to account for the bifurcation, the belief in an independent world and the felt boundaries of mind inside the head or at the surface of the sensory organs. Why do we believe mind stops at the ears and eyes and the world outside is independent? It seems inconceivable that this marvelous universe, which has existed for billions of years before we were born, and will continue well after we are gone, is merely an image of a true reality from which we are forever screened, a reality we will never know. Yet everything we see and hear and feel and think and believe — mind in its entirety — is brain activity. This does not mean there is no external reality, only that it is known through its model in the mind. The reasons for the belief that the world of sight and sound is independent of the observer are manifold but they bear enumeration and discussion.

Development: The paradigm for mental development is mitosis, division within a membrane. In mind, the first division is subject and object, which is a psychological mitosis within the subjective field of the organism. The object, or objective world, does not so much confront the subject as it draws outward and objectifies a portion of a subjective ground. This creates an objective and subjective segment within a subjective field. The subject responds to an outside world that is an extension of its subjectivity. The individuation of subject and object is the initial phase. Gradually, within the subject-portion, a self individuates in opposition to the world and in relation to its own subjective content. At the same time, the object-portion undergoes further articulation. The appearance of proto-intentional, then intentional, goals still remain within the mind's outer garment. The separation of object from subject is a transition from mind to world over a continuous sheet of mentation. This occurs in a recurrent sequence from a subjective core to an objective surface that is constrained by sensation at successive points. It leads to an objectified image that represents or models a world that results from the pruning of maladaptive form driven by the impact of sensory data on an endogenous process of image-formation.

The impact of sense data: After activation to a phase of vigilance or arousal, a construct of the act- and object-to-be organized about the body midline sets the process in motion, keeps it on track and shapes unconscious precursors to their outcomes. Sensory data orient the incipient act-object at archaic formations in brain to an outcome in rational thought, veridical perception and adaptive behavior. After the initial phase, there is relative suspension of sensation as the construct passes to a space of dream, symbolic imagery and thought. This phase is propelled to conscious reason and adaptation. The gaining of reality, or the detachment of perception from the mind, requires sensory data at the endpoint of this micro-temporal development.

When sensory constraints are in abeyance and the world is still present, say when we close our eyes and the visual data that impinge on the brain are reduced, earlier phases in thought-development come to the fore. So long as there are auditory or other sense data to maintain an external world, these phases are rational and adaptive, as in contemplation, deliberation or sustained concentration. With a persistent relaxation of constraints, thought can range from creative imagination to daydream and fantasy. With sensory data markedly reduced or eliminated, as in sleep or sensory deprivation, there is dream, hallucination or psychosis. Sensation at the neocortical phase of the traversal is the final constraint on the emerging pre-object. Sensation is essential to the analysis and externalization of the pre-object. Otherwise, there is premature termination or an improbable route of actualization. Personal need must adapt to impersonal reality.

In normal perception, as inferred from pathology, the application of sensation through the geniculo-striate pathways partitions the developing holistic pre-object and its space to a fully objectified image distinct from antecedent process in the mind. The foreshortened, palpable subject-centered space of imagery, dream or hallucination that underlies a proximate space of object relations — the perimeter of limb action or the world of the infant — becomes the open-ended, infinite expanse of waking perception. The transition is so abrupt, the model so accurate, the passivity and detachment so complete that we believe the outer world to be the source, not the product, of the perception. The restriction of the analysis and exteriorization to the distal segment of the mental state cleaves the object from the self, from private thought and feeling, to create an external rim of mind filled with extra-psychic objects. But all it takes is a brief spell of vertigo as the world spins around the observer to remind one that the world before us is an image in the mind.

Stages in memory and perception: The initial phases of the mental state arise out of an instinctual core — the inherited repertoire of drive categories — to a phase of affective and experiential memories that shape conceptual feeling in the direction of perception. Early phases are felt as memorial, later ones as perceptual, but a memory is an incomplete perception and a perception is a memory specified to an object. The image transports the experiential past to the ongoing present. The same transition occurs in all domains of cognition, for example, when a word individuates a semantic category. At successive phases and with sensory guidance, whole-part shifts eliminate the potential irrelevance or mal-adaption of possible objects to outer conditions. The transition from a perception that is like a memory to a memory that is like a perception delivers the present of ongoing experience out of the past of its own infrastructure. The traversal of a pre-perception from phases of distant to recent memory embeds conceptual, experiential and affective knowledge within what appears to be a naked object. The conventional belief that perception precedes memory merely translates common sense to theory of mind. The natural impulse is to ask, how can we recall something before we perceive it? But if object-formation is parsed to a model of reality over an endogenous phase-transition, the object incorporates as its trace the memorial sequence through which it is realized. In forgetting, earlier phases in the object are recaptured. Memory is thinking to the extent it departs from perception and perception is memory to the extent it fails to reach a veridical endpoint.

Feeling in opposition to objects: We seem to attach and direct feeling to an object. The feeling is felt inside the person as an interior phenomenon communicated in speech and action but largely inaccessible to others, as their feelings are to us. Most people believe that feeling is associated to objects or derives from them, or that there is an external connection from self to object or other, but feeling in the object is part of what the object is, part of its becoming or the process through which it is realized. The impression of an external relation to objects comes from their outward movement and loss. This splits the object off as something external, leaving its affective tonality behind. The effect is to reinforce the separation of mind and object and support the belief that the world is not ours to create but is out there to observe, react to and experience, which of course it is, but not in the manner most people believe it to be.

If we ponder how object-worth or value is generated — the feelings we have for others, for animals, for things, possessions, memories — we come to understand that feeling is not applied to objects but *develops into them*. The intensity of feeling for memory, dream, the savoring of the past, the concept of memory as incomplete perception, all conform to the idea that as the memorial becomes the perceptual, the affect that accompanies the image distributes as value into objects. Feeling is more intense at early phases of drive and desire, less so at distal ones of object and word-production. Moreover, feeling is felt as a pressure behind, directed or in opposition to the object, not in it. The process that leads outward from concepts to objects accompanies a specification of drive to desire, to affect ideas, feelings of interest and then outward in the externalization of the object as value or worth. The qualitative change over successive phases is continuous from activation to termination. Feeling is the vitality and becoming of the object and the mark of its realness.

Mind arises in experience of the world: The mind is not a *tabula rasa,* but to the extent it is so conceived, it is a tablet on which letters are carved in relief by chipping away at mal-adaption or redundancy. Instincts and primitive categories of knowledge form part of the animal endowment. The enrichment of mind through instruction and experience seems inserted from outside. The diversity of the world is not felt to be created by the observer but exists for enjoyment or suffering, in any event, to be perceived, absorbed, felt, stored and digested. There is a powerful impression of mind as a container filled by experience rather than sensation shaping the mind to conform or adapt to what is experienced. The reflection of the physical world is taken for the real. The creativity trimmed away in each cycle of world-creation is attributed to the internal portion of mind before the world appears. The incessant novelty that is the work of nature — the astonishing creativity of life — in the novelty of perception is a tributary of creativity in the mind.

Extension, causality, space and time: One of the earliest objections to a conflation of the mental and physical concerns the extension of external space. We know there are levels of space formation in the mental state, such as the space of dream, the space of the body, that of the newborn and congenitally-blind, so that an extended three-dimensional space, along with its objects, is achieved out of earlier space-forms. External space is elaborated over a transition in which an initial non-spatial field of insubstantial mind is set in opposition to the extensive space of a substantial world.

Subjective time, duration and the virtual present preclude instantaneity and differ from objective time-order and the causal sequence of world events (Bohm, 1980). The causal interaction of external objects is observed but not felt unless there is impact by an external cause, while action willed by the self is felt but not observed. We perceive causation in the world and feel it in the mind. When we act on a decision, it is not the decision that instigates the action but the self that feels an agent to the act. Decision is not the cause of action, no more than options that are blocked, abandoned or exhausted are the cause of inaction. In conscious thought we are informed of acts that are instigated at unconscious phases. For the most part, the direction of world events is from cause to effect, that of mental events is from potential to actual or from possibility to commitment. In the world, fact is primary and mind-independent, though influenced by probability and contingency. In the mind, possibility is the ground of freedom and fact is the final stage of belief. Consciousness involves a trajectory from self to object, and thus mediates a transition from the simultaneity of the unconscious to the temporal order of world events. The discovery of transitional phases in the *creation* of temporal order undermines a sharp opposition of these two frames of time-experience.

Transience and permanence: The inner perception of time and the outer perception of space, the feeling of transience in the mind, the coming and going of mental phenomena, the evanescence of life generally, the passing of things mental and the endurance of things physical, the stability of objects, the insubstantiality of thought, all combine to set one world against the other. All things are in change, indeed, it is intrinsic to them, but the tree in my garden will outlast my thoughts about it, the telephone will be there long after my conversation is over, and the generic cows in the meadow will replicate themselves long after my individuality is lost. Stability is the iteration of like-objects; impermanence is the iteration of dissimilar ones. It is a matter of the perceptibility of change and the repeatability of occasions. But, the tendency of mind to apprehend the extremes rather than the gradations accentuates these distinctions and makes overcoming them all the more difficult.

Evolution and cognition: The pillars of evolutionary thought are abundance of form and elimination of the unfit as the environment trims away and prevents the reproduction of less-fit organisms. Adaptation entails a pruning of organism so only those best-fitted to the environment survive. The population dynamic of evolution is realized in the micro-transition of the mental state. The environment in the form of sensation trims away irrelevant or mal-adaptive possibilities so what survives —an act, a thought, an object—is best suited to its social or physical habitat. The world of the organism, like that of object-formation, is a limiting point on degrees of freedom. The aim of evolution to produce and reproduce an organism best adapted to some niche in the physical world is the same as the aim of thought to produce and reproduce (replicate) an object best adapted to a momentary niche in the physical world. Both processes lead to an objectification and a continual re-testing of fitness.

Agency and recipience: An essential aspect of the indifference of the world to individual mind and the feeling that the objects that grow out of us to be independent of their conception is the transition from agency to recipience (passivity) in the outward-going flow. The feeling of agency is that of a self that wills an action. This feeling is conveyed into an action to give it a volitional character. Agentive feeling deposits in the body, not the world. I do not raise the glass—that would be telekinesis—rather, I move my hand which then raises the glass. An action belongs to the agent because it remains in the body and does not fully externalize. In object-development, intermediate phases prior to detachment may have a volitional quality. I can will a mental image to occur and *manipulate* it as I like. The image is *my* image. It has not fully separated. In instances of incomplete object-development, agency can be carried outward with the image, as in hallucinatory voices that command actions by the percipient observer.

Endogenous phases that actualize an image are guided by sensory data to veridical objects. There is progressive loss of voluntary control, which is ceded to terminal sensory constraints, finally to the world. As the image detaches and is felt to be independent of the perceiver, the agent becomes passive to the outcomes of his own image formation. The feeling of passivity to objects is essential to detachment, but agency is dependent on the nature and the phase of the content it accompanies. Agency can be lost or regained in pathology, as when an individual feels that objectified thoughts are transmitted to others. The differing modes of agency in various forms of mental imagery—after-images, eidetic images, memory images and so on—illustrate a transition from the voluntary to the involuntary in the passage outward to objects.

Knowledge and insight: We are constantly guided by knowledge of the world, especially the pragmatics of life, much of which is attributed to the cumulative wisdom of common sense. Common sense draws its considerable authority as a tactic for coping and survival that, by genetic or cultural transmission, has passed down over the ages. The perils attached to ignoring common sense have, no doubt, eradicated most of the outliers who raised questions about it or acted in a way as to deny what seem to be obvious truths. When applied to behavior in the world, common sense is a reasonable strategy. The difficulty arises when such beliefs are transferred to a theory of the mind, or become a standard against which theory is judged.

Much of microgenetic theory is a challenge to common sense beliefs, though the theory can explicate their origins. The problem occurs when a common sense theory of the world is interiorized as a theory of mind, or of antecedent phases in the mental state, or when early phases or constituents in perception are described in terms of final ones, or the flux of brain activity is depicted from the standpoint of external solids, or when memorial or unconscious contents are held to be copies of what is selected by consciousness. That a model of the real should grow out of fantasy, that objects are recognized before they are consciously perceived, that the world is an extension of the mind, that succession in time is generated out of simultaneity, or that the pathology of cognition displays preliminary normal phases, is not common sense dogma.

This brief introduction describes some of the phenomena that account for our experience of reality and the bases for believing, indeed, rarely questioning, the naïve view that the real world is just as it appears before us. We have learned that fact in the world is appearance in the mind, and that the phase-transition in the actualization of the world, as revealed by pathological conditions and altered states, is a continuum over neural and psychic substrates, not a sudden break from mind to nature. The notion of the unconscious and the perceptible world as *physical* spheres surrounding a psychic arena of consciousness is refuted by the perturbations of neuropsychology that expose phases that fill the process from unconscious to conscious and from consciousness to the world. The psychic landscape before me is not an hallucinatory vision but a representation of reality, though not the reality it represents. This changes little for me unless, like a schizophrenic, I *feel* the phenomenal basis of conscious experience, in which case the model, in its incompleteness or distortion, is exposed for what it is and life becomes intolerable. To know the real is inaccessible is an intellectual challenge or limitation, but to *feel* it is unreal is to live in the transition from dream to wakefulness.

Apart from an entrapment in the mind, the temporal extensibility of physical entities, as inferred from that of the mental state, entails that knowledge of a thing is knowledge of the change by which the thing exists. This means that being is not a frozen substance or slice but a becoming, a before and an after, that brings the thing into existence. It is probable that uncertainties at the quantum level in physics, or ambiguities that cannot be resolved by calculation, or do not obey some of the laws that underlie prediction, can be attributed to the temporal extensibility of nature, compounded in the mind, and the inability to escape the psyche regardless of the instrumentalities that are employed. A slight but significant error will occur owing to the approximation of mind to reality, or to the psychic process through which reality is encountered. We study the reality given in mind, not a reality mind can perfectly measure, for even in the most accurate representation there is inevitably some immeasurable disparity.

Glossary

MENTALITY:

The state or quality of mental or intellectual ability; a way of thinking.

NOVELTY AND CREATIVITY:

Novelty is uniform and universal newness in change. Creativity is an intermittent accentuation of novelty. *Novelty* applies to the fundamental nature of all change in organic and inorganic entities. *Creativity* refers to originality in artistic, scientific or other modes of thought. Originality or innovation and like terms describe modes of creativity.

SENSIBILITY AND SENSATION:

The term *sensibility* used in some philosophical discourse is preferable to sensation, which is often used interchangeably with perception. Sensibility differs from sense data, which are presumed to go into the formation of perceptions. Sensibility is extrinsic sensation, the physical impact of the world on the mind/brain but not a constituent of mind/brain process.

ENTITY AND OBJECT:

Entity refers to mind-independent things or events. Object refers to mind-dependent things or events. Perception is for objects and events. Entities are not perceptual objects.

MICROGENESIS:

The recurrent actualization of a series of phases from inner core to outer surface that mediates every act of cognition. The process develops in relation to phylogenetic stages in forebrain evolution, and is retraced in the growth patterns of ontogeny. Every traversal from onset to termination constitutes an absolute mind/brain state and an indivisible epoch of duration.

REALITY AND THE REAL:

Material or mind-independent reality comes to us through sensibility, constraining perception to a more or less accurate model of the external world. Survival depends on the accuracy of the model, which is off-line with physical passage or the progression of nature in space-time. Altered perception in dream or psychosis can still be felt as real. The feeling of realness is not the perception of reality, which is impossible.

CAUSATION:

Of the various notions of causation, this discussion centers on the presumed certainty of an event given a complete knowledge of its cause. On this view, causation is equivalent to universal determinism, and applies to all organic and inorganic entities as the means of passage in the world. Mental or agent causation is reduced to causation in the brain.

Index of Names

Subject Index